From Your Friends At **The MAILBOX**

SEPTEMBER

A MONTH OF IDEAS AT YOUR FINGERTIPS!

PRESCHOOL– KINDERGARTEN

WRITTEN BY

Deborah Burleson, Marie E. Cecchini,
Ada Hamrick, Lucia Kemp Henry, Suzanne Moore,
Mackie Rhodes, Karen P. Shelton

EDITED BY

Lynn Bemer Coble, Ada Hamrick, Jennifer Rudisill,
Karen P. Shelton, Gina Sutphin

ILLUSTRATED BY

Jennifer Tipton Bennett, Cathy Spangler Bruce,
Pam Crane, Lucia Kemp Henry, Susan Hodnett,
Sheila Krill, Barry Slate, Donna K. Teal

COVER DESIGNED BY

Jennifer Tipton Bennett

www.themailbox.com

©1996 by THE EDUCATION CENTER, INC.
All rights reserved.
ISBN# 1-56234-131-6

Manufactured in the United States
10 9 8 7 6 5

TABLE OF CONTENTS

September Calendar

National Better Breakfast Month

During September take the opportunity to emphasize to your students the importance of a nutritious breakfast. Throughout the month, provide pictures of nutritious breakfast foods. Vary the pictures each day so that the four food groups are represented. Discuss the pictures with students. Ask them to tell about some of the nutritious foods they eat for breakfast. Encourage youngsters to make healthy food choices for all their meals. As a related activity, provide magazines, scissors, glue, and a paper plate for each student. Have him cut pictures of nutritious foods from the magazines, then glue them on his plate. Encourage each child to show and tell his family about his plate of healthy foods.

Library Card Sign-Up Month

Join the effort, sponsored by the American Library Association, to have every child sign up for a library card during the month of September. For each day of the month, read aloud a story to your students. Send home a short note telling the title and author of the book read that day. On the note, include a brief sentence encouraging parents to look for that book in the library. Periodically remind them that September is Library Card Sign-Up Month. Suggest that they obtain library cards for their children while visiting the library.

4—First Kodak® Camera Patented

The first roll-film camera, registered in the name Kodak®, was patented by George Eastman on this date in 1888. His camera was equipped with enough film to produce 100 round pictures. As a result of Eastman's efforts, photography was made inexpensive and the camera became more popular. To commemorate this special occasion, take snapshots of the students and adults in your class. Mount each picture in a construction-paper frame with a circular mat cut from the front. Display the framed pictures on a back-to-school or Open House bulletin board.

7—Birthdate Of Grandma Moses

Anna Mary Robertson Moses, better known as Grandma Moses, was an American painter born in 1860. At the tender young age of 78, Grandma Moses began her painting career. On her 100th birthday, New York proclaimed this day to be Grandma Moses Day. She lived to the age of 101. After inspiring your youngsters with the story of Grandma Moses, encourage their creative instincts by providing them with a variety of paints, art paper, and applicators such as brushes, sponges, and brayers to use in their next art activity.

(Turn the page for more...)

3

10—Swap Ideas Day

Encourage little ones to share their thoughts and creativity by having them swap ideas with one another today. Gather several blocks to take to circle time. During this time, explain to students that today is a special day—"Swap Ideas Day." In turn, invite each child to tell and show an idea he has on how the blocks can be used, such as to build a bridge, to make music, or to create a fence. As children interact during play and center times throughout the day, encourage them to exchange their ideas with one another.

12—Birthdate Of Jesse Owens

During a college track meet, James Cleveland (Jesse) Owens broke five world records and tied a sixth—all within 45 minutes! During his lifetime, this American track-and-field athlete set 11 world records in the events of sprinting, hurdling, and jumping. At the 1936 Olympic Games in Germany, he won four gold medals. Owens's accomplishments gained him great admiration and made him a model for many young Americans. Set up a track-and-field course so your future record breakers can practice their skills. For fun, time each child as he runs a designated distance, or measure the length of his standing jump. At the end of the events, award each child a gold medal.

22—Ice-Cream Cone Patented

On this date in 1903, a lemon-ice vendor named Italo Marchiony filed for a patent for the ice-cream cone. His first cone was made of paper! To celebrate the birth of the ice-cream cone, have an ice-cream party. Before the celebration, have each child make and decorate a cone-shaped party hat. Invite him to wear his hat as he enjoys a delicious scoop of ice cream served in a cone.

24—Birthdate Of Jim Henson

The creator of the Muppets®, Jim Henson, was born in Missouri on this day in 1936. Best known for his puppets on the educational show "Sesame Street®", Henson's creativity has been recognized by the receipt of numerous awards. The Muppets® characters, particularly Kermit the Frog®, Big Bird®, Bert and Ernie™, Oscar the Grouch®, and Miss Piggy®, are familiar to children and adults alike. After reading a book featuring any of the Muppets® characters, provide old socks and a variety of craft items for students to use to create their own unique puppets.

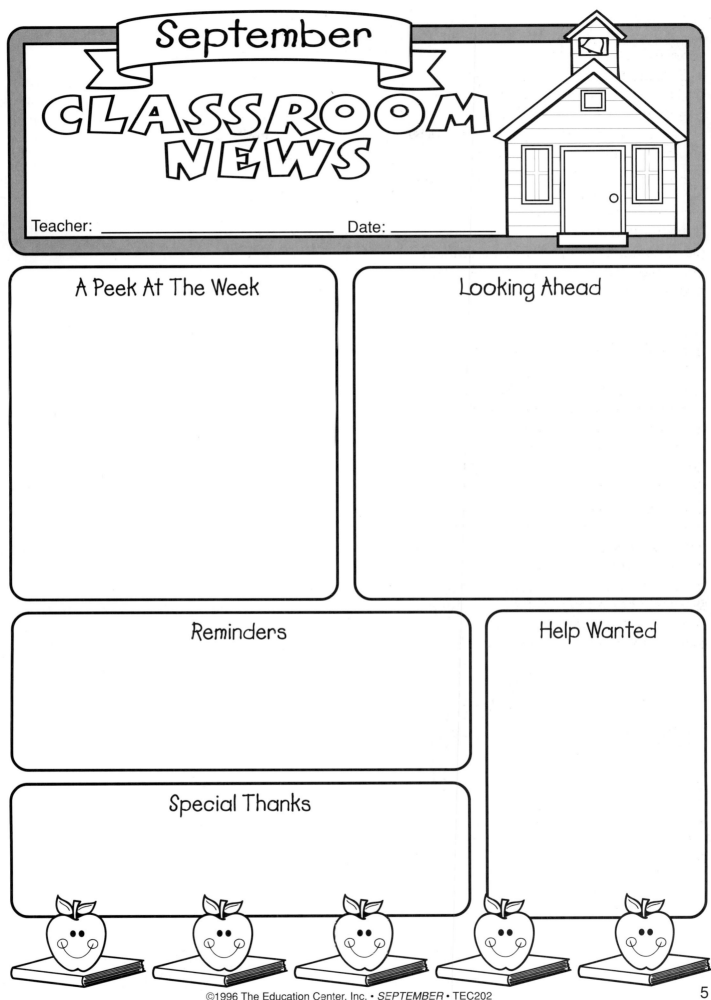

September

CLASSROOM NEWS

Teacher: _____ Date: _____

A Peek At The Week

Looking Ahead

Reminders

Help Wanted

Special Thanks

CELEBRATE!

20 Ways To Make Birthdays Special Days

THE BIG PICTURE

Picture this—a birthday message on your classroom door for all to see! Begin by bringing in a supply of birthday party hats and blowers for everyone in the class. Have everyone pose together—with hats on and blowers in hand—as a volunteer snaps a photo. Have the photo enlarged; then laminate it for durability. On each child's birthday, post the photo on your door, along with a message that reads "Happy Birthday, [Child's Name]!"

BIRTHDAY VEST

Purchase a child-sized denim or cotton twill vest in a solid color. Use slick fabric paints and glitter to decorate the vest with a birthday theme. Hang the vest on a hook in your classroom. When a child has a birthday, she may wear the vest over her clothes for the day.

PERSONAL POSTER

Create a poster of personal information for each child on his birthday. Print "Happy Birthday, [Child's Name]!" at the top of a sheet of 12" x 18" construction paper. Then use several colors of markers to record information about the birthday child, such as his favorite color, favorite food, family members, or favorite activities at school. Solicit compliments from classmates to write on the poster as well. Display the poster in the classroom for the day. Then roll it up, tie it with a ribbon, and allow the honoree to take it home.

BIRTHDAY BAKERY

On each child's birthday, transform your art area into an imaginary bakery. Stock the center with several colors of play dough, cookie cutters, birthday candles, rickrack, plastic knives, spatulas, cookie sheets, and cupcake papers. Youngsters may visit the center at free-choice time to make cookies, cakes, and cupcakes in honor of the birthday child.

A PARTY HAT PRIZE

At the beginning of the school year, purchase enough party hats for your class. As each child memorizes his birth date, present him with a hat to wear and take home. When all the children have learned their birthdays, celebrate with a class birthday cake!

Betsy Thompson—Gr. K • River Oaks Baptist School • Houston, TX

SINGING STAMP

Here's a musical treat that's hard to beat! Check your local gift shop for Talking Stamps™ from All Night Media, Inc. Purchase their rubber stamp with a birthday cake design that plays "Happy Birthday To You!" when it's pressed down. On each child's birthday, color over the rubber design on the stamp with a washable marker in a bright color. Press the stamp onto the child's hand (or a sheet of paper), and watch her eyes light up as the song plays! (You can order the stamp from Rubber Stamp Zone by calling 1-800-993-9119.)

©1992 ALL NIGHT MEDIA, INC
SAN RAFAEL, CA 94901

BIRTHDAY BANDANA

Here's a quick and easy way to distinguish the birthday child. Purchase some fabric with a birthday design, such as balloons or party streamers. Cut a 15-inch square; then fold the square in half to create a triangle. Use a permanent marker to write a message such as "Happy Birthday!" or "It's My Birthday!" on one side of the triangle. On each child's birthday, allow her to wear this bandana around her neck, with the birthday message showing in back.

A POCKET BOOK OF BIRTHDAYS

This special birthday book will be a big hit with your little ones. Begin by making 12 paper pockets. For each one, fold a sheet of 9" x 12" construction paper in half. Glue the two resulting six-inch sides together, leaving a pocket opening across the top. Staple the 12 pockets together along the left-hand side. Label the front of each pocket with one month of the year. Then take an instant photo of each child. In the white space below the image area, print the child's name and birth date. Place the photos of all the children whose birthdays fall in a particular month inside the corresponding pocket. Encourage students to "read" the book to find out who has a birthday in each month. If the photos get mixed up, the book becomes a sorting and matching activity.

glue

glue

pocket

David

January 3rd

January

PUT ON A HAPPY (BIRTHDAY) FACE

Use child-safe face paint to paint a simple design (such as a bunch of balloons) on the birthday child's cheek. Be sure to have a mirror handy so the honoree can enjoy this very special treat!

A BIRTHDAY NAP

Collect several cassette recordings of birthday-theme storybooks. At rest time on a child's birthday, give him the privilege of choosing a story for the class to listen to during this quiet time.

BIRTHDAY T-SHIRT

A birthday boy or girl will receive lots of special attention when he or she wears this birthday T-shirt. Purchase a plain, white T-shirt in an adult size Small. Use slick fabric paint to write "Happy Birthday To Me!" on the front of the shirt and "Hug Me! It's My Birthday!" on the back. Decorate around the messages with fabric paint and glitter. Each child may wear the shirt on her birthday. Children with summer birthdays may take turns wearing the shirt during the first week of school.

Jill Thaler—Gr. K • Little River-Academy, TX

BIRTHDAY BRACELET

Here's an easy-to-make treat for a birthday child. Cut a bracelet-length strip of brightly colored construction paper. Decorate the strip with birthday-theme stickers. Laminate the bracelet, if desired. Fit the bracelet to the birthday child's wrist; then staple or tape the ends in place.

"IT'S MY BIRTHDAY!"

Honor the birthday child with a special badge. Cut a birthday cake or cupcake shape from brightly colored Con-Tact® paper. Use a permanent marker to write "It's My Birthday!" on the cutout. Peel off the backing and stick it to the birthday child's shirt. The honoree is sure to receive many birthday greetings!

THE BIRTHDAY BAG

Use fabric paints to decorate a canvas tote bag with a birthday message and a simple design, such as balloons or birthday candles. Inside the bag, place several birthday-theme storybooks, activity pages, or puzzles. Have the birthday child choose a book from the bag for you to read to the class. Then invite him to enjoy the materials inside the bag at free-choice time or to take the bag home overnight.

Betsy Elder—Gr. K
Sutherland Public Schools
Sutherland, NE

TREAT TREE

This three-dimensional birthday display will brighten your classroom all year long. To make a treat tree, paint a small tree branch white. Place the branch in a bucket of plaster of paris and allow the plaster to harden. Then make a construction-paper cupcake for each child in your class. Label the front of each child's cutout with her name and birthday. Tape a small treat, such as a pack of gum, to the back of each cutout. Punch a hole at the top of each cutout, thread a length of yarn through the hole, and tie the yarn into a loop. Hang all the cutouts from the tree branch. On each child's birthday, have her find her cupcake and enjoy the treat.

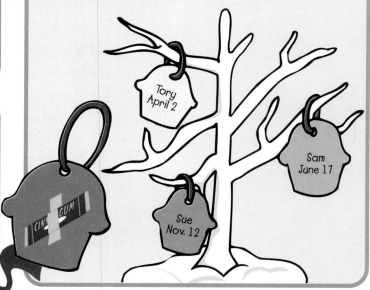

A COMPLIMENTARY CASSETTE

The birthday child will enjoy listening to this special cassette tape over and over again. On each child's birthday, place a blank cassette tape in your tape recorder. Record the whole class singing "Happy Birthday To You!" to the honoree. Then record each classmate giving a compliment to the birthday child. Place the completed tape into a tape box decorated with birthday-themed stickers. Send the tape home for the child and her family to enjoy.

A VERY SPECIAL VISOR

Looking for a birthday treat that's tops? Create a birthday visor for each of your little ones to wear on his special day. Purchase a plastic visor from your local craft store. Use a paint pen or permanent marker to write "Happy Birthday" across the visor; then add birthday-themed stickers, glitter, and imitation jewels. (Be sure to clean the visor thoroughly between each wearing.)

BIRTHDAY BUBBLES

Here's a "soap-erior" idea for celebrating a birthday! On each child's special day, provide bubble solution and a variety of bubble wands for the children to use during outdoor playtime. Everyone will look forward to birthday bubbles!

THE GREAT BIG BIRTHDAY BOOK

Use a chart tablet to begin a giant birthday book at the beginning of the school year. As each child celebrates his birthday, turn to a new page of the tablet. Print the birthday child's name at the top and add a school photograph. Invite each student to dictate a sentence about the birthday child. Then have the honoree illustrate the page. This giant book is bound to become a favorite with your youngsters!

Patt Hall—Gr. K
Babson Park Elementary
Lake Wales, FL

Courtney

Courtney has pretty eyes.
She likes to read.
Courtney's favorite food is tacos.
Courtney is a good runner.

Tommy

likes to play football.
to ride his bike in the
orite food is pizza.
good basketball

BIRTHDAY BANNER

Display birthday greetings in a big way with this cooperatively constructed banner. On separate sheets of 9" x 12" construction paper, draw the outline shape of each letter in the message "Happy Birthday, [Child's Name]!" On each of two separate sheets of paper, draw the outline of a birthday object. Distribute one of the programmed sheets to each of your students. Ask each student to color the letter or object and write her name below it. Glue the completed sheets of paper together along the edges to create a banner. Display it in the classroom or hallway for the birthday child's special day; then roll it up and let the honoree take it home.

HAPPY BIRTHDAY, SAM!

Jon Doug Mike Reba Vicki Ena Don David Kim Susan Todd Owen Seth Amber Keith Tonya Beth Steve

CAKE-AND-CANDLE DAYS

Start the school year on a joyful note by focusing on a familiar experience for your little ones. *Real* birthdays may come only once a year, but invite everyone to participate in this birthday theme full of ideas to span the curriculum. "Happy learning to you; Happy learning to you;…"

by Ada Hamrick

Who's Having A Birthday?

Your students are sure to ask who's having a birthday when they see a decked-out classroom on the first day of your birthday unit. Put students in a birthday mood by hanging party streamers from the classroom ceiling and adding a few well-placed balloons*, a "Happy Birthday" banner, some brightly wrapped packages, and a copy of the birthday-party announcement (on page 14) at each child's seat or cubby. Your excited students will be happy to learn that they're all invited to join in the birthday celebration!

Begin by sharing the story *Happy Birthday, Dear Duck* by Eve Bunting (Clarion Books). Then give each child an opportunity to relate a story about a special birthday. Ask children to compare Duck's birthday party with their own experiences.

(*Please note: Uninflated balloons create a choking hazard for small children. Keep them out of the reach of youngsters.)

You've Come A Long Way, Baby!

Once you've introduced your birthday unit, you'll have the perfect opportunity for noting each person's growth and how he has changed from year to year. Share the story *Birthday Presents* by Cynthia Rylant (Orchard Books) to help illustrate this concept for your youngsters. After reading the book, ask youngsters to talk about the many changes—physical, mental, and emotional—they have experienced since they were babies.

Then send home copies of the note on page 14 asking each family to provide a baby picture of their child. Create a bulletin board or wall display with the title "Birthday Babies." Display each baby picture side by side with a current photograph of the child. Write each child's birth date on a sentence strip and attach the strip below his pair of pictures. Give the display an interactive quality by stapling flaps of paper over the current photos. Students can try to guess the identity of each baby, then lift the flap to check. Little ones will delight in seeing the changes in themselves and their classmates since "babyhood"!

BIRTHDAY BABIES

May 7   August 15

October 2   September 21

A Birthday Chant

Do your little ones know their birth dates? Teach them this fun chant to help them remember this important bit of personal information. Seat students in a circle on the floor. Remind each child of her birth date before beginning. (You may want to give each child a sentence strip with her birth date printed on it to prompt you during the activity.) Explain that when you call a particular month, all children born in that month may stand and cheer. (Vary the number in the third line for your age group.) Say the chant that follows:

[September] birthdays,
Stand up and cheer!
[Six] bright candles
On your cake this year!

Repeat the first verse of the chant until each month has been called at least once. When students seem familiar with their birth months, add to the activity. Repeat the chant for a particular month and ask the children who "stand up and cheer" to remain standing. Have the group say the second verse of the chant (below) once for each individual child who is standing. Each standing child may then say her birth date. When all the birthday children for a particular month have responded, let them sit down and start over with another month.

When is your birthday?
What's the date?
We know you can hardly wait!

Birthday Keepsakes

Bring in an instant camera to prepare a birthday surprise for each child. Put on a birthday hat and invite each student to do the same. Ask each youngster in turn to pose with you while an assistant or parent volunteer snaps a picture. Don't show these developing photos to the students; tell them the purpose for the photos is a surprise. Then duplicate and program a copy of the birthday certificate on page 15 for each child. Attach the corresponding photo in the space provided and sign your name. On each child's birthday, present him with his certificate as a birthday memento.

HAPPY BIRTHDAY
to Tonya
From: Mrs. Albright
Date: September 9

11

A Cake Of Many Colors

What would a birthday celebration be without a cake? Read *The Birthday Cake* by Joy Cowley (The Wright Group), the story of a colossal cake fit for a queen. (This big book is available from The Wright Group. Call 1-800-523-2371 for ordering information.) The story's simple text follows two bakers as they build a cake with layers of different colors. After sharing the book, invite students to practice color recognition as they tell their own versions of the story on a flannelboard. Duplicate the cake-layer pattern on page 15 several times on tagboard. Color each cake layer a different color, including all the colors you'd like your students to learn. Laminate the cake layers for durability and cut them out. Affix the hook side of a piece of Velcro® to the back of each cutout. Have students build their multilayered cakes on a flannelboard, identifying each color as they work. For more advanced students, print the accompanying color words on sentence strips and attach the hook sides of pieces of Velcro® to the backs of those as well. Have students place the correct color word beside each cake layer on the flannelboard.

Wrap It Up!

After you serve the cake, it's time for—presents, of course! Most children delight in opening gifts on their birthdays. But while many have experience at unwrapping gifts, they may find wrapping them more of a challenge. Stock a gift-wrapping center to encourage practice of fine-motor skills and co-ordination. Ask families to donate empty boxes, birthday-themed wrapping paper, bows, ribbon, and cellophane tape. Given scissors and a large work area, your little ones are bound to get all wrapped up in this activity!

It's In The Cards

Little ones like to receive birthday cards almost as much as they like birthday presents. Recycle some birthday cards for new uses in a Birthday Card Basket to help youngsters practice a variety of skills. Ask parents to send in old or unused birthday cards, or purchase some inexpensive cards with different designs. Cut off the back flaps and discard them. Laminate the card fronts for durability.

Students can sort the cards, circle letters or words on them using a grease pencil, copy the text, match them to correctly sized envelopes (if available), or use them for lacing practice. (To create a lacing card, punch holes around the perimeter of a card. Thread a shoelace through one hole and secure it with a knot.) If you have enough cards, write one child's name on the back of each card. Students can then "deliver" the cards by matching the child's name on the card to the name on her cubby or desk.

HAPPY BIRTHDAY

Birthday Matchups

Gather a variety of birthday items for this fun game to help students practice visual memory. In advance, collect matching pairs of several birthday-related objects. You may wish to include two party hats, two gift bows, two birthday invitations, two birthday candles, two party blowers, and two balloons. Tape each individual item to a separate square of tagboard. Show the students all the pairs before you begin. Then ask several volunteers to stand in front of the group. Give each volunteer a tagboard card to hold, instructing him to keep it turned so that the birthday item cannot be seen.

The remaining students then take turns guessing which two volunteers are holding each matching pair of items. During his turn, a child may call two volunteers' names. Those children turn their cards around so that everyone can see what items they are holding. If the items match, the teacher takes those cards. The child who guessed correctly may have a turn to hold a card in the next round. If the items do not match, the cards are turned back around and another child may guess.

Donna Cox—PreK
Waterbridge Elementary
Orlando, FL

¡Feliz Cumpleaños!

Party hats, cake and ice cream, a special meal—most families have their own special ways of celebrating birthdays. Introduce your young learners to the birthday traditions of one Mexican-American family by reading *Hello, Amigos!* by Tricia Brown (Henry Holt and Company). Help your students practice saying, "Happy birthday," in Spanish—*"Feliz cumpleaños."* Then have students help you fill a piñata purchased from a party supply store. Save the piñata for a birthday celebration to culminate the unit (see "It's Party Time!").

It's Party Time!

Put on the party hats once again and welcome youngsters to a birthday bash for everyone! Invite some parents to join you to help supervise the festivities. Purchase or have parent volunteers donate unfrosted cupcakes. Allow each child to frost a cupcake and add colored sprinkles and a birthday candle. If fire codes permit, light each child's candle and allow it to burn while everyone sings "Happy Birthday To You!" After your little revelers blow out the candles, let them eat the cupcakes with scoops of ice cream on the side. If your students helped to fill a piñata (see "¡Feliz Cumpleaños!"), consider inviting a special guest, such as your school principal, to break it open. Then settle things down by reading the silly story *Moira's Birthday* by Robert Munsch (Annick Press Ltd.). Conclude the party by giving each child a small present, such as a birthday sticker or stamp.

Birthday Announcement

Use with "Who's Having A Birthday?" on page 10.

Parent Note

Use with "You've Come A Long Way, Baby!" on page 10.

Dear Family,
    At school we are learning about birthdays. Could you help by sending in a photo of your child as a baby? If you have a picture taken on your child's actual birth date, that would be wonderful! Don't forget to label the photo on the back with your child's name. We'll return it as soon as we're done with our activity.
                Thank you!

HAPPY BIRTHDAY

to _____!

From: _____

Date: _____

Attach photo here.

Cake-Layer Pattern
Use with "A Cake Of Many Colors" on page 12.

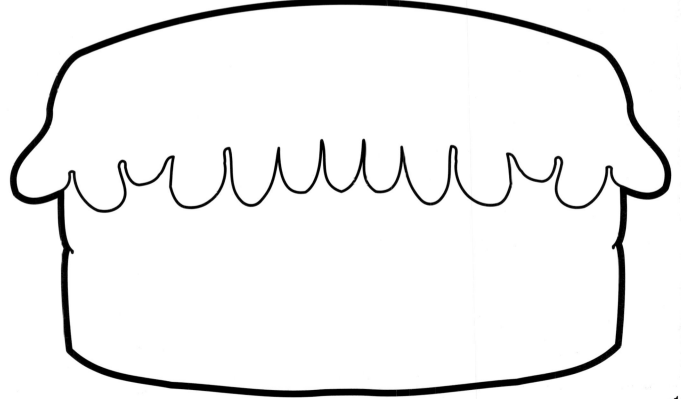

Me, Myself, And I

With these activities that emphasize each child's unique characteristics and abilities, your youngsters will develop an awareness of the identities that exist within each of us—me, myself, and I.

by Mackie Rhodes

Me

Since self-awareness lies in each child's knowledge of his own physical being, engage your youngsters in some "Me-ology"—the study of me.

Moveable Me

To help reinforce your little ones' awareness of their own bodies, perform some vocabulary-building exercises with this song about moveable body parts. Ask children to point to each body part named as they sing. Invite them to move creatively as they sing the last line of each verse.

(sung to the tune of "B-I-N-G-O")

My arms have parts that bend and move
Every time I use them.
Shoulder, elbow, wrist, and hand.
Shoulder, elbow, wrist, and hand.
Shoulder, elbow, wrist, and hand.
And this is how I move them!

My legs have parts that bend and move
Every time I use them.
Knee, ankle, heel, and foot.
Knee, ankle, heel, and foot.
Knee, ankle, heel, and foot.
And this is how I move them!

My trunk has parts that bend and move
Every time I use them.
Neck, back, waist, and hips.
Neck, back, waist, and hips.
Neck, back, waist, and hips.
And this is how I move them!

I'm made of parts that bend and move
Every time I use them.
Shoulder, elbow, wrist, and hand.
Knee, ankle, heel, and foot.
Neck, back, waist, and hips.
And this is how I move them!

A Mystery Put To Rest

Whew! After all the activity in "Moveable Me," your youngsters will be ready for some rest and a little suspense. Have them sit or lie very still. Explain that their *outer* body parts—the parts of our bodies that can be seen—began to rest as soon as they stopped moving. But wait! Has everything *inside* their bodies begun to rest too?

Take this time to investigate some of the mysterious happenings inside our bodies. Help each child find his heartbeat by placing one hand on the left side of his chest. What makes that thumping? Is the beat fast or slow? Next have him place a hand along the side of his neck to feel for the pulse of his jugular vein. Also show him how to use his index finger to find the pulse on his wrist. Do these areas thump also? What causes the pulse in his neck and wrist?

Next encourage each child to place his hands on his chest. What causes that movement of his chest? How does it move when he breathes in? Out?

Conclude by telling youngsters that the outsides *and* insides of our bodies are made of fascinating, moveable, and usable parts. Mystery solved: case closed.

The Long And Short Of Me

There will be no shortage of interest or learning with this body awareness activity. Cut a three-foot-long piece of bulletin-board paper for each child. Spread the paper out on the floor. Have the child sit on the edge of the strip and stretch one leg out as far as possible over its length. Use a marker to trace the outline of his leg; then write the words "my leg" above the outline. In the same fashion, make and label an outline of his arm, hand and foot, lining each

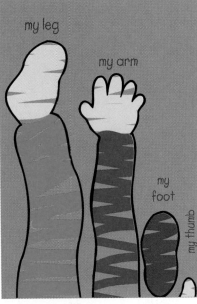

part up at the same edge of the paper. Allow the child to choose more body parts to trace as space allows—a finger, a thumb, or even a toe. After drawing all the outlines, have the child color them. Using the resulting picture graph of his body parts, encourage him to compare their lengths. What a lengthy subject our bodies are!

Give Me A Hand

Your students will applaud themselves with this "handy" self-portrait made from—what else?—their own handprints. Reproduce the head pattern on page 22 for each child. Provide trays of blue, green, brown, yellow, red, and black finger paints. Using the paint that corresponds to the color of her eyes, have each child press one fingertip into the paint, then fill in the eye color on her picture using her fingerprints. With the paint representing the color of her hair, encourage the child to use her hand- or fingerprints to fill in the hair on her self-portrait. When the paint dries, allow the children to embellish their portraits with skin colors, freckles, teeth, eyeglasses, and hair ornaments to further personalize the self-portraits. What a handsome group of kids! For an extension of this activity, see "I'm A Poster Child" on page 21.

"Sense-sational" Me

R-r-r-rip. Sniff. Br-r-r. Mmmm! Tickle and tantalize the senses with this stimulating cooking project that will make your youngsters take notice of their senses and how they work together. Purchase enough flavored-gelatin mix to make one serving per child. With the help of your students, plan to make the gelatin using the speed-set directions on the box. Use the provided lists of suggestions to guide your children in using their senses in each step of the preparation. When the gelatin has chilled, the students will be ready for yet another "sense-sational" experience—eating it!

What The Children...

- **See:** the powder and water colors; the shape and size of the ice; the change in the powder and water when mixed; the movement of the mixture as it is stirred; the appearance of the mixture as ice is stirred in; the appearance of the chilled gelatin
- **Hear:** the box and inner wrapper being opened; the powdered mix, water, and ice being poured into the container; the mixture being stirred; the chilled gelatin being scooped with a spoon
- **Smell And/Or Taste:** the powder, water, and ice; the liquid and chilled gelatin mixture
- **Feel:** the dry powder; a drop of warm water; a piece of ice; the temperature of the container as warm water and then ice are added and stirred together; the movement of the liquid during stirring; the temperature and texture of the gelling and the chilled gelatin

Keisha

Myself

A young child needs to feel comfortable not only with her own physical being, but also with her ability to *act on* her physical world—to manipulate and control things in a positive, functional manner. With these self-focused activities, your little ones will be quick to share their confidence and independence with others.

I Can Do It By Myself

Let Mercer Mayer's Little Critter® help your youngsters sing their own praises about their daily accomplishments. Read the humorous, but self-affirming, *All By Myself* by Mercer Mayer (Western Publishing Company, Inc.) to your class. After sharing the story, have a discussion about all the things Little Critter® can do by himself. Also talk about the things that he may still need a little help with, such as tying his shoes, pouring a drink, and getting settled for bed. Assure your children that it is alright to have help with things that they are just learning how to do—because before long they will be doing these things by themselves, too. Then read the story again, this time adding the question, "Can you?" to each statement made by the character. You will delight in the choruses of "Yes, I can!" and the proud faces that accompany these affirmations.

The Myself Express

Now that your little ones are loaded with pride, let them steer The Myself Express to the land of I Can for a chance to toot their own horns. To begin, attach to a child's wagon a banner with the words "The Myself Express." In a designated area of the room, place a sign that reads "I Can—The Land Of No Limits." Then, on an adjustable baseball cap, tape or pin a card with the phrase "I Can." During circle or center time, let each child have a turn to wear the cap and pull the wagon around the land of I Can to gather toys, clothing, and other materials that he can manipulate by himself. Instruct him to make three or fewer selections. When the child has made his choices, have him pull The Myself Express back to the terminal (the circle or center area) to demonstrate all the things he is able to do with no help. Listen to his horn blow, "I Can, I Can, I Can," as his confidence kicks into high gear!

All By Myself

Use this catchy tune to give your little ones a way to express the pride they feel in their many achievements. Make up actions to go along with the words as you sing.

(sung to the tune of "Three Blind Mice")

All by myself.
All by myself.
See what I can do!
See what I can do!
I can brush my teeth and my hair so neat.
I can put my socks and shoes on my feet.
I can get my napkin and snack to eat.
All by myself.
All by myself.

All by myself.
All by myself.
See what I can do!
See what I can do!
I can clean up my toys, I can ride my bike.
I can kick a ball and match pictures alike.
I can read a book and sing songs that I like.
All by myself.
All by myself.

A Clean Image Of Myself

Your students will be bubbling over with a clean self-image when they participate in this sudsy drawing activity. To make a bubble-bath mixture, combine 1/3 cup of water and one cup of bubble-bath powder. (A mild powder for children, such as Mr. Bubble®, is recommended.) Whip the mixture into a foam with a wire whip or an eggbeater. Supply a learning center with framed mirrors, the container of whipped bubble-bath foam, and plenty of damp paper towels. Then have each child look into a mirror to examine his reflection. Instruct him to dip his finger into the foam and trace the features from his own reflection onto the surface of the mirror. To conclude, help the child recite, "Mirror, Mirror, who can this be? *[Pause.]* I drew myself. It's a picture of me!" Rub-a-dub-dub the surface of the mirror with a damp paper towel to clean it off for the next child.

My Mouth And Myself

Lipreading is made easy when you use these mouth puppets to help your little ones express and validate their feelings. For each child, cut two short lengths of dark-colored yarn and two construction-paper mouths. Have him color each of the mouth cutouts. Next glue a piece of yarn onto one of the cutouts to create a smile and onto the other to make a frown. Then attach the back of one of the cutouts to a Popsicle® stick. Flip the stick over and attach the back of the other cutout so that it lines up with the first one. When finished, each child will have a happy-/sad-mouth puppet. He may hold his smiling mouth up in front of his own mouth as he takes a turn telling about a situation that makes him happy. Then he can flip his puppet over to show the sad mouth as he recounts a sad situation.

... And I

"I have a pet lizard," "I like red the best," and "I want to be a paleontologist when I get big," are only a few of the numerous statements heard in a class of young students. Every child has the need to tell about himself and to discover how he *fits into* his physical world. Your youngsters will enjoy the opportunities to share their ideas about themselves and their world with the activities in this section.

I Want The World To Know

News flash! We interrupt this program to bring you a very important person. With the use of this television learning station, your little citizens can air their personal opinions. Locate a box that is approximately 24 inches high and wide. To convert the box, cut away the top flaps and one of its sides. Cut a large square from the opposite side using an X-acto® knife. (This opening will serve as the television screen.) Paint the box; then turn it over so that the bottom becomes the top of the TV. Decorate the box to resemble a TV set by drawing knobs or dials along one edge of the screen. Attach two long pipe cleaners in a V-shape to the box to represent antennas, if desired. Place the television set on a table.

Have a child position himself behind the box so that his face can be seen through the screen of the TV. Encourage each child to role-play a television anchorperson by having him tell the news about himself. Guide him to tell his name, age, and birthday; the names of his family members; where he lives; what he likes and dislikes; his favorite toys, games, and shows; places he likes to go; and so on. Place a tape recorder nearby to record each child's program. To extend this activity, replay the taped interviews at a later date, and have the children share any new or different information about themselves.

I Am Many Things

Our moods and perceptions about ourselves take on a variety of forms. Read the book *Quick As A Cricket* by Audrey Wood (Scholastic Inc.) to your students. Then discuss with the children the many different ways they perceive themselves. Read the book again—this time encouraging the children to act out the idea expressed on each page. Then, to give additional opportunities for self-expression, let your youngsters mold play dough into various shapes, forms, and animals to depict their emotions and perceptions. Using *Quick As A Cricket* as a guide, have each child project his own perceptions onto his creation by stating, "I am as [name a characteristic] as a [name of the creation]." For example, he may create a model of a bee and then say, "I am as busy as a bee." Or he may say, "I am as cuddly as a bear," in reference to a bear he created.

I've Got Rhythm

Call attention to the uniqueness of each child's name with this rhythmic name game. To begin help each child learn the rhythm of her name by clapping out the syllables and counting each beat. For example, for the name *Jessica,* the child will clap three times and count, "1, 2, 3." To play, have the children listen as you call out a verse; then have them do as the verse directs. As play continues, call out the verses at random so that the children must listen carefully to know when to respond. Do you have the rhythm? Can you keep the beat?

If your name has a beat—*(pause; then clap one time)*—a beat of one,
Call your name out loud; then run, run, RUN!

If your name has a beat—*(pause; then clap two times)*—a beat of two,
Call your name out loud; then jump like a kangaroo!

If your name has a beat—*(pause; then clap three times)*—a beat of three,
Call your name out loud; then buzz around like a bee!

If your name has a beat—*(pause; then clap four times)*—a beat of four,
Call your name out loud; then crawl across the floor!

If your name has a beat—*(pause; then clap five times)*—a beat of five,
Call your name out loud; then put your body into drive!

What I Like

Initiate a brainstorming session with your class using the book *What We Like* by Anne Rockwell (Macmillan Publishing Company). As you read each page, encourage your children to name some of the special things that they like. Then, by gluing pictures from magazines and catalogs onto a sheet of construction paper, encourage each child to form a collage in similar fashion to the pages in the book. Program the top of each child's page to read "What [child's name] Likes." Laminate each of these pages; then assemble them into a class book titled "What We Like."

I'm A Poster Child

Make your little ones the main attraction with these boaster-posters. To begin let each child make the self-portrait described in "Give Me A Hand" on page 17. Duplicate pages 23, 24, and 25 for each student. Ask a parent volunteer to cut out and assemble the pages into a poster for each child. Have each student bring to school a photograph of himself doing something he enjoys, such as feeding a pet or eating pizza. (If a photograph is not available, he may cut a picture from a magazine.) Instruct him to color the body section of the self-portrait using his favorite colors. Next show him how to glue his photograph between the child's hands on the poster. Then help each child complete the statements on page 25 as you write his responses on the lines. When each child's poster is completed, display it in a prominent place.

21

Use with "Give Me A Hand" on page 17 and "I'm A Poster Child" on page 21. When using this with "I'm A Poster Child," glue bottom of picture over indicated area on page 23.

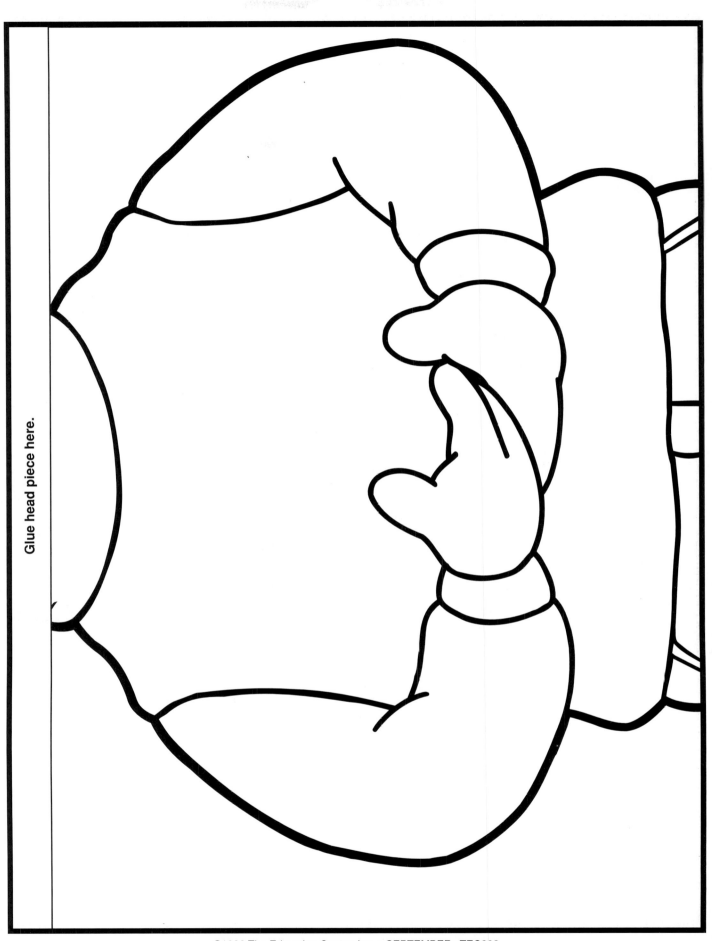

Glue head piece here.

Use with "I'm A Poster Child" on page 21. Glue bottom of picture over indicated area on page 24.

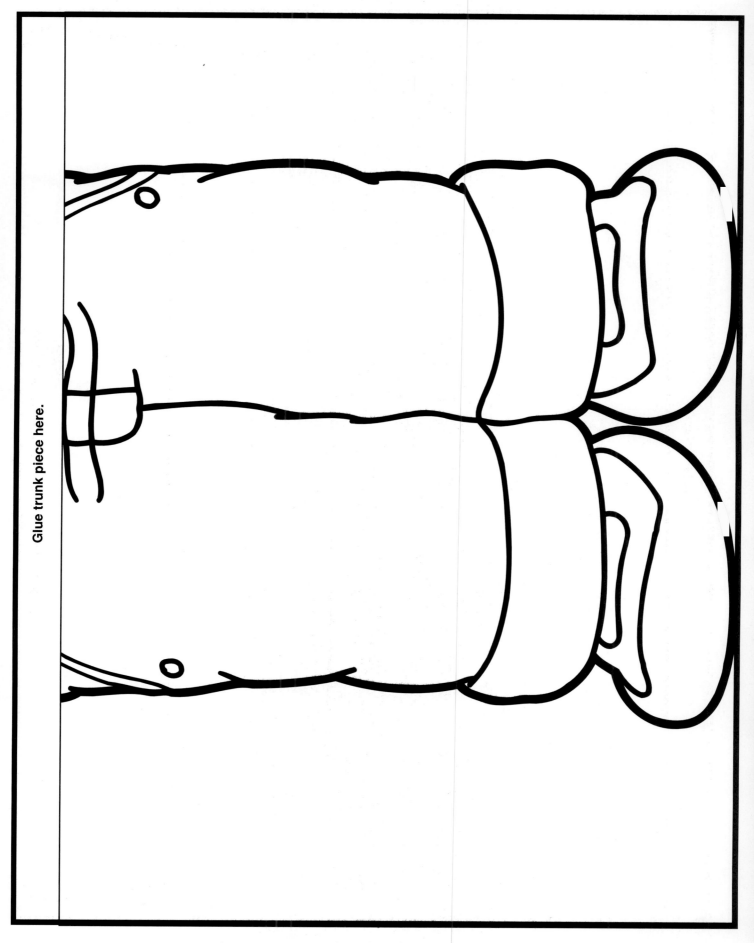

Glue trunk piece here.

Use with "I'm A Poster Child" on page 21. Glue bottom of picture over indicated area on page 25.

Meet Me

My name is _____

I like to _____

My favorite color is _____

I can _____

by myself.

©1996 The Education Center, Inc. • *SEPTEMBER* • TEC202

Use with "I'm A Poster Child" on page 21.

You've Got To Have Friends!

For many children, September means a new school year and new friends. With the ideas in this friendship unit, get your youngsters off to a great start by creating a classroom climate of kindness, sharing, and cooperation.

by Lucia Kemp Henry

Make A New Friend

Help your youngsters get to know each other with this simple cooperative activity. On white construction paper, reproduce the Puzzle Pals patterns on page 32 so that there will be one puzzle piece for each student. Use markers to color each puzzle pair with a distinctly different pattern or color. Laminate the patterns; then cut along the bold lines to cut each pair apart. Punch a hole near the top of each puzzle piece and thread a long piece of yarn through the hole. Tie the ends of the yarn to form a necklace.

Before school starts one morning, place a Puzzle Pal necklace in each child's cubby or at his seat. Encourage students to wear their necklaces. Give each youngster time to locate the wearer of the matching Puzzle Pal—his partner for the day. Ask each child to introduce his new friend to the class by saying, "This is my friend [insert child's name]." As this pair of students moves to a designated space (for forming a large circle), encourage everyone to sing "The More We Get Together." Repeat this entire cycle until every child has been introduced and all students are forming one large friendship circle.

The More We Get Together

The more we get together,
    together, together.
The more we get together,
    the happier we'll be.
'Cause your friends are my friends
And my friends are your friends.
The more we get together,
    the happier we'll be!

What Is A Friend?

Help your youngsters think about what *friendship* means by asking them to brainstorm a list of descriptive words to complete the sentence, "A friend is...." Write the student-dictated words on cards, and display them on a wall or bulletin board. Using white construction-paper Friend Figures duplicated from pages 34 and 35, have each youngster create a self-portrait. Instruct each youngster to cut out his figure; then arrange the figures near the word cards so that they appear to be holding hands.

What Is A Friend?

A friend is ...
kind.
Daniel

Good Friends

To help children understand what kinds of behaviors make someone a good friend, teach your youngsters this poem. Later your little friendship experts may want to add some new stanzas of their own.

Good Friends

Good friends are so nice to have
When we work and play.
Good friends are awfully kind.
They help along the way.

Good friends say, "Hello," or "Hi!"
When they meet each day.
Good friends can take your coat
Or put your boots away.

Good friends like to help with blocks
When you have too many.
Good friends share their crayons, too,
When you don't have any!

Good friends help clean a mess
That's spilled upon the floor.
Good friends like to let you in
When you are at the door.

Good friends play a game of catch
Or make a jump rope turn.
Good friends show you how to play
If you want to learn.

Good friends say, "Thanks for your help!"
And say, "I'm sorry," too.
Good friends say, "I'm so glad
To have a friend like you!"

Jeremy shared his crayons with Ellie.

A Special Someone

After learning the "Good Friends" poem and seeing some of the behaviors in action, your students will be able to talk about what it means to be a friend. Take time each day to have youngsters tell you about friendly things they have seen people doing. Keep a list of these positive behaviors on chart paper and refer to them often. You can also review them as possible solutions to unresolved classroom conflicts.

Have your youngsters make a big book that features some of the friendly behaviors that they have seen or that they have performed. Ask each child to draw a picture that shows someone doing something "friendly." Write each youngster's description of her illustration in the remaining space on her paper. Staple all of the pages together beneath a construction-paper cover. Title this class booklet "Friends Do Special Things."

Friendship Songs

Begin and end your busy day with these songs about friendship.

Good Morning, Friends
(sung to the tune of "Row, Row, Row Your Boat")

Hi! Good morning, friends.
How are you today?
Let's each try to be a friend
To everyone today!

Good-Bye, Friends
(sung to the tune of "Are You Sleeping?")

Good-bye, friends. Good-bye, friends.
Time to go. Time to go.
Thank you, friends, for helping.
Thank you, friends, for sharing.
Love you so! Love you so!

Our Friendship Goals

Foster a sense of cooperation, acceptance, and togetherness in your classroom by focusing on positive, friendly behaviors. Keep a camera handy so that you can photograph your youngsters when they are cooperating or working well together. Display these photos on a permanent bulletin board that you add to throughout the year. You may find that you'll have lots of youngsters who are quite proud to be caught in the act of being friends!

Our Friendship Guidebook

Conflict Resolution

To aid in conflict resolution, select your youngsters' top three or four typical conflicts. Photograph your students in the midst of acting out each of these disagreements in turn. Then photograph them demonstrating several possible solutions to each of these conflicts. Display these photos on a bulletin board. Later, when similar conflicts arise, youngsters can refer to the photos for possible solutions. When they feel more competent at conflict resolution management, transfer the photos to an album titled "Our Friendship Guidebook." You may be surprised to see how many youngsters refer to the guidebook instead of opting for an unsuitable alternative.

Friendly Words

Involve your youngsters in the establishment of a positive classroom climate by having them brainstorm a list of friendly words to use every day. Before beginning, help them understand the difference between friendly and unfriendly words. Talk about how some words make people feel good or happy when people say them. Other words have the opposite effect. Write the brainstormed words on construction-paper cards and display them in a pocket chart. Use these words in the chant below.

Friendly words, friendly words,
Use them every day.
Friendly words, friendly words
Feel so good to say.
[Chant your list of brainstormed words.]

kind   happy   nice

friendly   helpful

The Doorbell Rang:
A Sharing Story

This wonderful book, written and illustrated by Pat Hutchins (Greenwillow Books), is just right for youngsters of different ages. The predictable format of the story is a magnet to budding readers, while the illustrations allude to the mechanics and mathematics of sharing.

After reading aloud the story, set up a similar scene for all of your youngsters to role-play. Provide two youngsters with enough tagboard cookie cutouts to equal one cutout for each child in your class—including yourself, if necessary, to keep the number of cookies even. Retell the story, making alterations as necessary, until there is one cookie per person...and the doorbell rings. If you wish to make this reenactment into a class book, photograph the students and their cookies as the retelling progresses. Later use the photos to illustrate your own version of the story.

During the days that follow this dramatization, divide students into small groups at snacktime. Then, for each group, provide a plate with twice as many crackers as people in the group. Have students work together to divide the snack evenly. On subsequent days, continue giving students opportunities to decide for themselves how to evenly divide the snack provided.

Hands Of Friendship

With a fine-tip black marker, carefully trace around each youngster's hands on a sheet of white construction paper. Let each youngster color in his handprints with a skin-toned crayon or marker. Write each youngster's name above his pair of handprints. Arrange all the children's handprints on a bulletin board so that they make a circle. In the center of the circle, attach a photograph of the entire class. Title the display "A Circle Of Friends."

Friendship Goals
Parent Letter

Program and duplicate the reproducible letter on page 33 to inform parents of your friendship goals and activities. You might suggest that children repeat the "Friendly Words" activity on page 28 with their parents or that they visit the library to find some books about friendship. Any way you choose to use page 33, the unspoken message will be that friendship, kindness, and cooperation are valued in your class.

Friendly Cooperative Fun!

Emphasizing cooperative games fosters friendship as well as fun! Try these whole-group games to focus on the importance of working together as a team.

Cooperative Hugs

Your classroom will be filled with friendly vibrations when your youngsters play this cooperative game. Begin by having your youngsters spread out within a large, open space. For safety's sake, be sure to emphasize that this is a walking game with no running allowed. Play a recording of some moderately paced instrumental music to accompany the game, or play an upbeat song with friendly lyrics such as the classic "You've Got To Have Friends" by Bette Midler. Play the music while youngsters dance around in place. When you stop the music, instruct *each child* to find *one person* to hug. Play the music again and have each pair of youngsters dance together. Stop the music again. This time have *each pair* of youngsters find *another pair* to hug. Then these *foursomes* can dance together until the music stops and they join *other foursomes* for a big hug. Continue in this manner until all your youngsters join together for one big friendly hug.

Make A Circle

This cooperative game is lots of fun to play and provides youngsters with an opportunity to develop their listening skills as well as their imaginations. Have youngsters spread out within a large, open space. Have them walk around quietly, listening for your signal. When you are ready, stand still and call, "Make a circle!" Your youngsters must move to where you are and join hands to make a circle around you. Do this several times—always moving to a different spot in the room.

When your students have mastered the basic circle-forming skill, throw in some simple variations. When you signal them, call something different such as, "Tiptoe into a circle!" or "Make a monkey circle!" (students move like monkeys once they are in the circle). Remind students that the circle must be formed around you each time.

The Friendship Train

This game is easy, but it takes quite a bit of cooperation to keep a string of little bodies all moving in the same direction! Have your youngsters spread out within a large, open area. Try this game a few times with an adult leader (the engine). Play some instrumental music softly in the background. Have the leader move toward one youngster. As the leader passes him, the youngster "hooks on" by placing his hands on her hips. Continuing from child to child, children continue to join the Friendship Train. The last child, or caboose, may then become the engine for the next game. If desired, make the game a bit more difficult by asking that youngsters build a train in boy-girl-boy-girl sequence.

Learning The Buddy System

Give each of your youngsters opportunities to work one-on-one with many different classmates by involving her in these partner activities.

Wear A Shirt

Gather a supply of long-sleeved, extra-large men's shirts. Ask for donations, or search yard sales and thrift shops for inexpensive castoffs. Make sure that you have enough shirts for every two youngsters. Group students in pairs and give one shirt to each pair. Explain that both people in each pair must "wear" the shirt together! Encourage students to come up with several different ways of doing this. After a while, have students select new partners and repeat the activity.

Buddy Crawl

Assign partners once again for this activity. Line up several sets of partners along one side of your play space. Instruct each pair to move to the opposite side of the play space together. Further explain that each person in each pair must be crawling and that the partners must remain in physical contact as they move. Youngsters can develop and try a number of different ways to accomplish this task. Some pairs may hold hands and crawl. Some may crawl side by side, keeping their torsos in contact. And some may crawl with one person leading while the other person crawls holding the leader's feet. Explain to students that this game is less of a race and more of a challenge to work together creatively.

Move A Hoop

Pair your students; then give each pair one plastic Hula-Hoop®. Ask each pair to step inside the hoop. Then instruct the pairs of children to move to a specified location. Explain that youngsters may move in any way, but they must both remain inside the hoop. Repeat the task a second time with the same partners to allow each pair to refine its communication and movement techniques. Later direct partners to jump, hop, skip, or otherwise move together inside the hoop to reach their destination.

Make A Shape

Provide each pair of children with a jump rope or six-foot length of heavy cord or rope. Hold up a sign bearing the outline of a square, circle, triangle, or rectangle. Have each pair work together to re-create the shape on the sign. Continue the activity, changing the outline to be copied.

Later you may want to include signs with more complex shapes such as an oval, a diamond, or a heart. Or you may want signs showing numerals or letters of the alphabet.

Friendship Puzzle Pals

Use with "Make A New Friend" on page 26.

Dear Parent,

Friend Figure
Use with "What Is A Friend?" on page 26.

34

HOW ABOUT HOUSES?

Move right into this across-the-curriculum collection of activities about houses. There's no place like home—for learning opportunities!

by Ada Hamrick

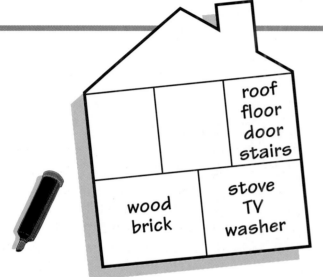

roof
floor
door
stairs

wood
brick

stove
TV
washer

A House Is...

Introduce your youngsters to the topic of houses and homes by helping them to construct an idea map. In advance, cut a sheet of poster board into a simple house shape. Use a marker to divide the house into rooms, as shown. Then show the cutout to your students. Tell them they are going to be learning about houses and homes. Ask them what ideas come to mind when they think about houses or the homes where they live. As children provide responses, write them inside the various rooms of your house cutout. Group the responses into various categories as you write. For example, one room might have a list of *types* of houses, while another room might have a list of *items* found in a house; yet another room might have a list of *people* who live together in a house.

When the lists are complete, direct students' attention to the various categories and review their responses. Point out that they already know a great deal about houses! Display the house cutout throughout your study with the title "All About Houses."

A Parade Of Homes

Near the start of your study, send home this family project to get parents and children working together. For each child, provide a sheet of poster board cut into a simple house shape. Send a poster-board cutout home with each student, along with a note asking the family to help the child decorate the house with their choice of art materials. Suggest some materials they might use, such as paint, markers, magazine pictures, pasta, fabric pieces, or photographs. Indicate a due date and look forward to some creative responses!

If some families are unable to help their child complete this project at home, allow time during the school day for those children to work on their house projects with an adult volunteer or a child from an upper grade. When all the children have completed their houses, allow them to share their creations with classmates. Then display the houses in the classroom or hallway, and invite parents in to view the "Parade Of Homes."

Who Builds A House?

While your youngsters are beginning their decorative houses at home, invite a carpenter to school to tell them about creating a *real* house. Ask your visitor to bring along samples of his woodworking or photos of a house or building under construction.

Prepare students for their visitor by reading *A Carpenter* by Douglas Florian or *Building A House* by Byron Barton (both published by Greenwillow Books). Before the visitor arrives, help the students formulate a list of questions they'd like to ask.

All Kinds Of Houses

There are many different types of houses all over the world. Introduce your students to some international homes with the book *This Is My House* by Arthur Dorros (Scholastic Inc.). Then have your little ones help you create an oversized graph showing their favorite houses. Enlarge the house patterns on page 42 to the desired size for a bulletin-board display. Have groups of students color the houses and mount them on a bulletin board. Then ask each child to vote on her favorite type of house and to explain why she finds that particular kind of house appealing. Place an index card with her name printed on it in a column above her choice of house. Count and compare the numbers of children who voted for each type of house. Add a title to the board that reads "Our Favorite Houses."

A Song About Shelter

Help your little ones learn about houses with this song and its accompanying movements. Discuss the basic parts of a house that allow it to provide shelter: *walls, roof, doors,* and *windows.*

Build A House
(sung to the tune of "Row, Row, Row Your Boat")

Build, build, build a house — *Make hammering motions.*

With doors and windows, too. — *Place palms together; then open them to imitate a door opening. Touch thumbs and fingers together to form a square window.*

Add a roof to keep it dry— — *Touch fingertips overhead to form a roof.*

A home for me and you! — *Point to "me" and "you."*

An Address Book

After learning about houses all around the world, help your youngsters concentrate on where they live. Help students learn their addresses with this class book they'll want to read again and again. Duplicate one copy of the house pattern on page 43 and program the house to read "Who lives at _____?" as shown. Then duplicate a copy of the programmed page on white drawing paper for each child. Fill in the blank on each child's page with his address. (Or have students write or copy their addresses if they are able.) Then have each child cut out his house shape and cut the door on the dotted lines as indicated. Glue each cutout onto a sheet of colored construction paper, but do not glue down the door. Fold open the door to each house cutout and glue a small photo of the child who lives at that address inside the house. Close the door by unfolding the paper. Bind all the pages together and add a cover with the title "Our Address Book."

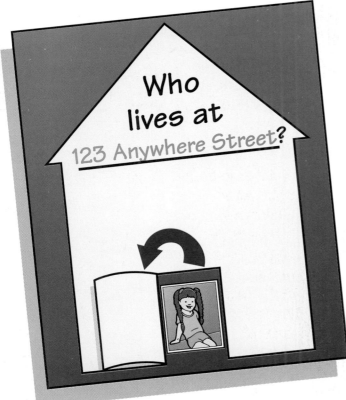

A Place For Everything

For more bookmaking fun, encourage little ones to create individual booklets of household items to help them practice sorting skills. Duplicate the booklet on pages 44 and 45 for each child. Cut the pages apart, assemble each child's booklet, and staple it together. Have students search for pictures of household items in old magazines and catalogs. Ask them to cut out pictures and glue them on the appropriate pages of their booklets. Create front and back covers for the booklets by cutting construction paper into simple house shapes. Print the child's name and the title "In The House" on each front cover.

Shapely Houses

This art and language activity will sharpen students' shape-identification skills as well. Read *My House* by Lisa Desimini (Henry Holt and Company). The eye-catching illustrations in this book will put students in an artistic mood. Provide students with a large supply of simple shapes cut from a variety of wallpaper designs. Include rectangles, squares, triangles, and circles. Encourage each of your little ones to choose and identify several shapes, then assemble them to create a house. Have him glue his design onto a sheet of white construction paper and add a scene around it with crayons. Review the illustrations in the story to remind students of what happened to the house as the weather and seasons changed. Below the house, write the child's dictation as he completes the sentence, "My house _____." Have the children share their finished houses with classmates.

My house is happy.

A Street Scene

Focus on another math skill—patterning—when you have students create street scenes with houses. Duplicate several copies of the house pattern on page 43 on various colors of construction paper. Laminate the houses for durability and cut them out. Back each cutout with a piece of magnetic tape or Sticky-Tac. Tape a few sentence strips in a row along the bottom edge of your chalkboard or along a wall. Tell little ones that the sentence strips represent a street, and they are going to "build" a neighborhood using the house cutouts. Then place some of the house cutouts along the street—creating a pattern as you work, such as green-blue-green-blue. Ask a student to continue your pattern as she adds more houses along the street. Repeat the activity with a different pattern; then invite students to create their own patterns.

House Numbers

Count on houses for more math practice when you invite students to create combinations of ten. Read *Anno's Counting House* by Mitsumasa Anno (Philomel Books). This wordless book depicts a group of ten children who move between two houses, creating various combinations that form a set of ten.

After discussing the story, invite students to explore combinations that equal ten with a manipulative math activity. For each child in a small group, duplicate two copies of the house pattern on page 43—each on a different color of construction paper. Laminate the houses for durability and cut them out. Also provide a set of ten manipulatives for each child, such as teddy bear counters or bingo chips (on which you've drawn faces with a permanent marker). Each child in the group may use his manipulatives to create combinations that equal ten. If desired, have youngsters record all the combinations they discover.

$3 + 7 = 10$

Houses, Houses Everywhere!

Extend the theme of houses and homes throughout your classroom with these ideas for enhancing your learning centers.

Block Area: Encourage students to work individually or in groups to build houses in your block center. Provide a variety of building materials, such as traditional wooden blocks, Lincoln Logs®, cardboard bricks, and LEGO® pieces. If possible, add toy trucks and simple machines such as levers or pulleys.

Sand Table: Provide sand-castle molds and containers in a variety of shapes for youngsters to use in creating sand structures.

Art Center: Cut painting paper into simple house shapes for students to use at the easel. Also provide clay, craft sticks, and pattern blocks for creating tabletop houses.

Woodworking Center: Set up a center with blocks of wood, toy tools, child-sized hard hats, and a variety of screws, bolts, and other hardware for students to explore. Provide adult supervision, and allow students to use toy hammers or wooden mallets to pound golf tees or nails into pieces of Styrofoam®.

Math Center: Use photos of houses from realty magazines as math manipulatives. Select clear, large photos; laminate them for durability; and cut them out. Place them in your math center and encourage little ones to use them for various math activities. Students can sort the houses by color, number of windows, garage/no garage, etc. They could also use the photos to count out sets or create patterns.

Science Center: Bring in some examples of animal homes for students to examine. Purchase a piece of honeycomb at a farmer's market, collect an abandoned spiderweb by spraying a sheet of black construction paper with hairspray and pressing it against the web, hunt for an unoccupied bird or wasp nest, and scoop an anthill into a large-mouthed glass jar. Display the homes in your science area, along with a book about animal homes, such as *Animal Homes:* part of the What's Inside? series (Dorling Kindersley, Inc.).

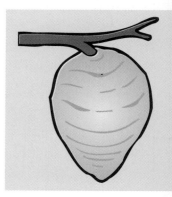

Reading Area: Place books with a house-and-home theme in your reading area for students' enjoyment (see the literature list on page 41 for some suggestions). Create a homey atmosphere by providing an upholstered chair, a rocker, or some comfy pillows. Add warm light with a reading lamp.

Housekeeping Center: This area naturally lends itself to the study of houses. Add to the usual fun by organizing a moving-day activity. Bring in empty boxes, a child's wagon, and a stack of newspaper. Have little ones wrap and pack the household objects into boxes and load all the boxes into the wagon. When the center is empty, rearrange the furniture. Then invite the youngsters to return to the area, unpack, and move into the new residence!

MOVING DAY!

This House Takes The Cake!

Celebrate the end of your study by building and eating this tasty structure! To create a house cake, bake cake layers in two square pans. When the layers are cool, cut one layer into three pieces as shown. Assemble the cake as illustrated and frost it. Have your little ones use a variety of cookie and candy items—such as graham crackers, vanilla wafers, miniature marshmallows, cereal pieces, or butter mints—to add features to the house. Add details, such as windowpanes, with tube icing. Your young architects will love digging into this delicious dwelling!

Is There A Good Book In The House?

Of course! Share these literature selections to build on your house-and-home theme.

A House Is A House For Me
Written by Mary Ann Hoberman
Published by Puffin Books

Goodbye House
Written by Frank Asch
Published by Little Simon

A House For Hermit Crab
Written by Eric Carle
Published by Picture Book Studio

The Little House
Written by Virginia Lee Burton
Published by Houghton Mifflin Company

The Maid And The Mouse And The Odd-Shaped House
Adapted by Paul O. Zelinsky
Published by Dutton Children's Books

Aren't They Grand?

Use the following activities during September—around Grandparents' Day—to help your children develop an awareness of the important role grandparents have in their lives. As their awareness is heightened, encourage youngsters to continually show appreciation and love for their grandparents and other older people.

For those students without grandparents (or students who have little or no contact with their grandparents) suggest that they might focus on an older neighbor, friend, or relative during these activities. Or consider "adopting" a nursing-home resident as a class grandparent.

ideas contributed by Marie E. Cecchini

Meet My Grandparents

Each and every grandparent is special in his or her own unique way. Because of this, each student will be eager to tell his classmates about his grandparents. Send a note to each child's parents mentioning your unit on grandparents and asking them to send to school a picture of their child's grandparents (or other older friends). Use Note 1 on page 53 for this purpose. When the pictures begin arriving at school, make two photocopies of each one and label the back of each photocopy with the corresponding student's name. (If desired, use a photocopier to reduce or enlarge the photos so that the photocopies are all about the same size. If clarity can be maintained, images that are about 8" x 10" will be especially effective with the suggested activities.) Place each photo in a labeled envelope for immediate return to parents. For each student who doesn't bring a photo, photocopy a picture of either an adopted grandparent or an older friend, or a magazine picture that somewhat resembles him or her.

Once you have two photocopies of each child's grandparent or older friend, randomly display each photocopy on a fabric-covered bulletin board bearing the title "Aren't They Grand?" Give each youngster an opportunity to tell his classmates about his grandparents. Later, when they have unstructured time, encourage students to locate several matching pictures on the board.

Unparalleled Pairs

If your students created the bulletin board described in "Meet My Grandparents," plan to reuse the pairs of photocopies to make Concentration-style matching games. If you did not create the bulletin board, obtain photocopies of grandparents' pictures as described in "Meet My Grandparents." Cut tagboard into a deck of cards sized to fit even the largest of the photocopies. Glue each photocopy to a different card.

To introduce your students to the game of Concentration, start with only two matching pairs of cards. Randomly place the cards facedown on a tabletop, and have students take turns touching the backs of the two cards that they believe are identical. If a match is not revealed when the cards are turned over, return them to their facedown positions and have another child touch two cards that he believes are identical matches. Each time you play the game, use an additional pair of cards to increase the difficulty level.

Puzzles With Personality

If you made the bulletin board described in "Meet My Grandparents" or the game cards in "Unparalleled Pairs," creating these puzzles will be a snap. To make one, you will need a photocopy of a grandparent's picture that has been glued to a tagboard card. Laminate at least one picture card for each student. Then cut each card into an appropriate number of puzzle pieces. Assign each puzzle a different numeral or letter; then program the back of each of its pieces with the assigned code. If the puzzle pieces become mixed together, students can re-sort the pieces using the codes. For storage, label a different string-tie envelope or resealable plastic bag with each code and place the corresponding pieces inside.

Family Trees

To begin this activity, read aloud *Grandma's Bill* by Martin Waddell (Orchard Books), which explains the child/parent/grandparent relationship. Then encourage students to create trees that aren't your typical family trees. Ask students to help you gather small parts of tree branches. You will need one tiny tree branch for each child. Once back indoors, have students assist you in making several batches of baker's clay (see the recipe below). When the clay is ready, have each child press some into a personalized margarine tub or plastic cup, then anchor his tree branch. Allow the clay to harden.

Meanwhile send copies of Note 2 on page 53 to parents, asking that they assist their youngsters in bringing small things to school that remind the children of their grandparents. As the items arrive at school, assist each youngster in attaching the objects to his tree. Finish the trees, if desired, by having students glue on bits of yarn or tissue paper for added color. As each youngster puts his tree on display, have him dictate a sentence or two telling why the things on the tree remind him of his grandparent(s). Write each child's dictation on a folded card and display it near his tree.

Baker's Clay
2 cups flour
1 cup salt
water
Mix flour and salt together. Slowly add as much water as necessary to make the clay pliable; then knead until smooth.

Grandpa Herb likes to fish. We fish together.
Luke

Grandma Hodnett likes to sew. The buttons remind me of her.
Katie

Granny Joyce likes to bake. We clip coupons together.
Katie

My Grandma is nice. She bakes me cookies.

Sharing Stories

Students who participate in the "Family Trees" project on page 47 can transition into this activity by discussing their trees. Whether or not students created family trees, they will be eager to talk about their grandparents. As each child has a turn, tape-record his answers to the following questions: What does your grandparent (or older friend) like to do? What kinds of things do you do with your grandparent? What makes your grandparent special? After each child has had an opportunity to be recorded, play the recordings during storytime. If desired, follow these stories with a reading of Mercer Mayer's *Just Grandma And Me* and *Just Grandpa And Me* (Western Publishing Company, Inc.).

Everyone Has Feelings

To prepare for this activity, gather a few magazine pictures of older people displaying a wide variety of expressions. Read aloud (or paraphrase) *Grandpa's Face* by Eloise Greenfield (Philomel Books). Afterward discuss the fact that Tamika's grandpa used a lot of different expressions because he was an actor. Hold up a magazine picture that shows happiness, despair, anger, worry, or silliness. Ask the children to identify the emotion involved. Have students pretend to be actors and imitate the expression. Provide a mirror so they can compare their expressions with the expression in the picture. Then talk about what types of things might cause this kind of expression and emotion. Explain that people of all ages experience similar emotions.

Ask your children what expressions they prefer to see on the faces of their grandparents (or older friends). Usually they will prefer happier expressions. Then encourage the children to think of things they can do to elicit happy expressions.

Looks Like Glasses Are In Order

Show students a few pictures of older people who are wearing glasses. Ask the children to decide what all the people have in common. Talk about the fact that many grandparents may need to wear glasses at least part of the time. Explain that spectacles are the same as glasses. Encourage youngsters to join in the following fingerplay.

Grandparents' Spectacles

Here are Grandma's spectacles.	*Circle fingers around eyes.*
Here is Grandma's hat.	*Form a cone shape on head with hands.*
And this is the way she folds her hands	*Fold hands together.*
And lays them in her lap.	*Rest hands in lap.*
Here are Grandpa's spectacles.	*Circle fingers around eyes.*
Here is grandpa's hat.	*Form a cone shape on head with hands.*
And this is the way he folds his arms	*Fold arms across chest.*
Just like that.	*Nod head.*

Wonderful Memory Boxes

For your students who have spent oodles of time with their grandparents, these boxes will be precious reminders of things they have done together. First have each student collect an assortment of paper items or nearly flat objects that represent some of the experiences he has shared with his grandparent. To inform parents, send home copies of Note 2 on page 53.

To make a memory box, cut a strip of bulletin-board paper just a little bit less in height than a shirt box. Accordion-fold the paper at intervals a little less than the width of the shirt box. Trim away excess paper at the ends of the strip. Unfold the paper. Have a student decorate the strip of paper to represent some of the times he has shared with his grandparent. Write each child's dictation as he describes the significance of each item. Tape one end of the paper inside the lid of the box and the other end inside the bottom of the box. Refold the paper and close the box. Have the child decorate the outside of his memory box before sharing it with his grandparent.

You may want to vary this activity for students who have spent less time with their grandparents. Have each of the students with less-involved grandparents collect an assortment of things that show what he has been doing. Assemble this memory box as before, and encourage the youngster to send or present it to his grandparent to bring him or her up-to-date.

My grandma and I got this stuff near the pond. The ducks quacked at us. Grandma said they wanted us to feed them.

Grandpa took me to the fair. My favorite part was when I won a goldfish.

Dad is teaching me to play ball. I'll be in the major leagues one day!

I love to see movies.

Caroline is my friend. We dive into leaves together.

Mom says I'm an artist.

Family Favorites

Some of the best family memories are related to foods or meals. Perhaps there's a story about the time Grandpa Shelton stuffed himself on Granny's fresh apple pies. Or maybe the family loves to recount how delectable Grandma Ruby's bread pudding is. At any rate, a cookbook featuring favorite recipes of grandparents and other older friends is bound to be popular. Duplicate copies of page 55 and send a couple of copies home with each student along with a copy of Note 6 on page 54. As the recipe pages start flowing into school, reproduce the pages so that each family will have a copy and so that the grandparents involved or mentioned can also have a copy. Complete each cookbook by duplicating the design on page 54 and gluing it to a construction-paper cover. No doubt this cookbook will be a best-seller!

Recipes & Memories
From Our Grandparents & Other Older Friends
Created by Mrs. Ryan's Class

This recipe was contributed by

This recipe makes people think of
because ...

recipe name

Ingredients

Directions

Hug Card Pattern
Use with "Marvelous Messages" on page 49.

Fold.

I love you this much!

Fold.

©1996 The Education Center, Inc. • SEPTEMBER • TEC202

Note 1—Picture Request Reproducible
Use with "Meet My Grandparents" and "Unparalleled Pairs" on page 46, and "Puzzles With Personality" on page 47.

Note 2—Memento Request Reproducible
Use with "Family Trees" on page 47 and "Wonderful Memory Boxes" on page 51.

Could we borrow a picture?

We will soon be talking about grandparents at school. So that your child will be prompted to participate by talking about his or her grandparents (or other older friends of his or her choice), we'd like to borrow a photograph of them. Please label the photo so that we will know to whom to return it. Once the photo arrives at school, we will make photocopies of it and use the copies in one or more activities. Your photo will be returned as soon as we have made our copies.

Please send a photo of one or more grandparents or older friends by _____.
(date)

Thank you for helping make our grandparents unit a success!

We need your help!

At school, we are planning two projects honoring grandparents and other older friends. Please help your child think of small items that represent the interests of one or more of his grandparents.

For example, if one grandparent lives by a fishing pond, a few fish-shaped crackers could be sent to school. Or if your child has a grandparent who likes to sew, small squares of fabric could be sent to school. Perhaps your child appreciates the fact that his grandparent takes him to the movies. If so, you might want to send ticket stubs and a movie advertisement to symbolize that shared activity.

These items will not be returned, so please help your child choose carefully.
Please try to have the items at school by
_____. Thank you!
(date)

Note 3—Contacting Grandparents Reproducible
Use with "Marvelous Messages" on page 49.

Note 4—Note To Grandparents Or Older Friends
Use with "Marvelous Messages" on page 49.

Could you supply an address?

As a part of our grandparents unit, your child has an opportunity to send a message to one or more of his or her grandparents (or other older friends). He or she will send a card and a request that the grandparent reciprocate by sending a note to the child. If you would like your child to participate, please address one or more envelopes to the appropriate grandparents and return them to school. We will make each greeting card at school, stamp the envelope, and include a note asking the grandparent to mail a note to the child at school.

Please return the addressed envelopes tomorrow. Thank you for your help!

In this envelope you will find a hug. It was made especially for you by _____.
(name)

Our class would really like to hear from you. Please write us a note if you can. We would like to learn something about you and the area where you live. (Maybe you could send us a postcard.)

Enjoy your hug, and write to us if you can!

Class name:

_____

School Address:

_____

_____

_____

Note 5—Gift Tag Reproducible
Use with "Worth Their Weight In Gold" on page 50.

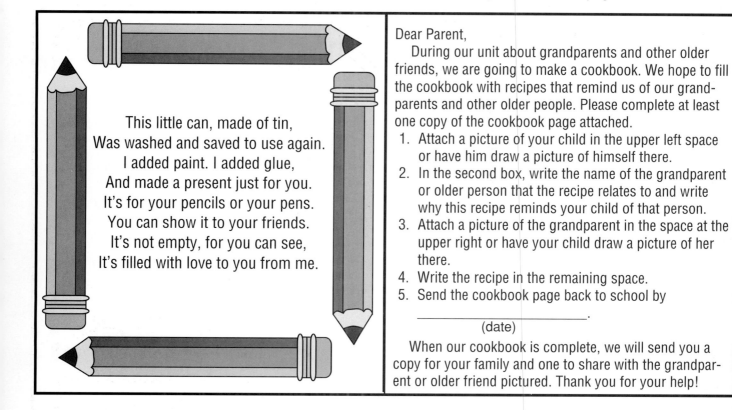

This little can, made of tin,
Was washed and saved to use again.
I added paint. I added glue,
And made a present just for you.
It's for your pencils or your pens.
You can show it to your friends.
It's not empty, for you can see,
It's filled with love to you from me.

Note 6—Information About Blank Cookbook Page
Use with "Family Favorites" on page 51.

Dear Parent,

During our unit about grandparents and other older friends, we are going to make a cookbook. We hope to fill the cookbook with recipes that remind us of our grandparents and other older people. Please complete at least one copy of the cookbook page attached.

1. Attach a picture of your child in the upper left space or have him draw a picture of himself there.
2. In the second box, write the name of the grandparent or older person that the recipe relates to and write why this recipe reminds your child of that person.
3. Attach a picture of the grandparent in the space at the upper right or have your child draw a picture of her there.
4. Write the recipe in the remaining space.
5. Send the cookbook page back to school by

_____
(date)

When our cookbook is complete, we will send you a copy for your family and one to share with the grandparent or older friend pictured. Thank you for your help!

Cookbook Cover
Use with "Family Favorites" on page 51.

Recipes & Memories

From
Our Grandparents
&
Other Older Friends

Created by

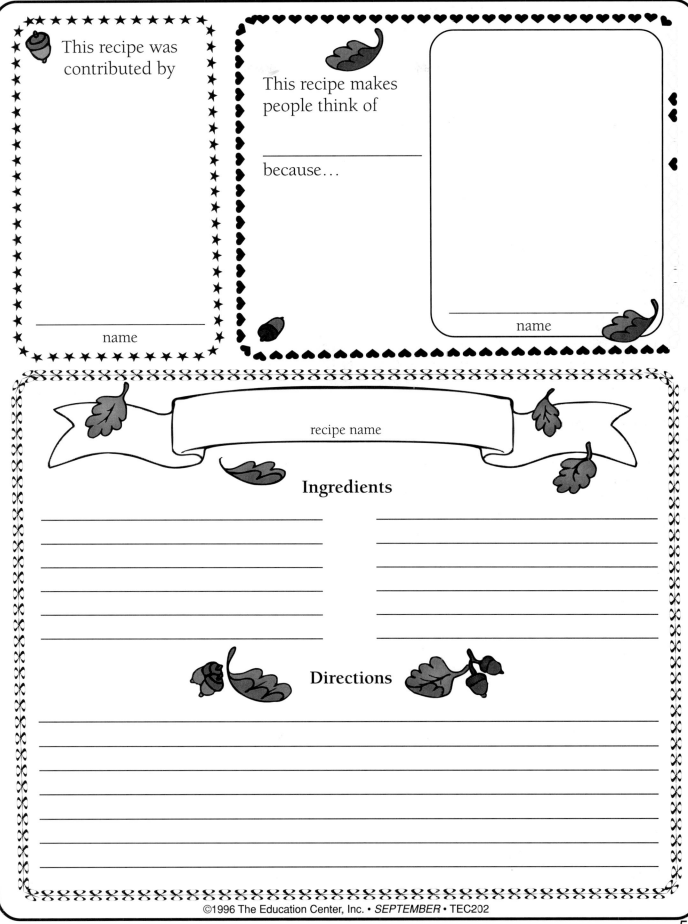

This recipe was contributed by

_____
name

This recipe makes people think of

_____

because…

_____
name

recipe name

Ingredients

Directions

Apples Aplenty

Pick some or all of these "a-peel-ing" apple activities to share with your little ones. An apple a day will bring learning their way!

by Ada Hamrick

A is for APPLE

Investigating Apples

Get right to the core of your apple study by bringing in a basketful of real apples. Include several different varieties. Invite youngsters to examine the apples up close. Encourage them to sort the apples by various attributes such as color, shape, or size. Cut open several of the apples, slicing some parallel and some perpendicular to the core. Have students examine the insides of the apples and discuss what they see and smell. Cut a few of the apples into pieces for your children to taste.

After the apple exploration, ask students to brainstorm words or phrases to describe apples. Responses might include *red, green, full of seeds, round, white inside, sweet,* or *crunchy.* Write the students' responses on a large apple shape cut from poster board or bulletin-board paper. Display the apple cutout throughout your study.

Math In Good Taste

While you have those apples handy, conduct a taste test to determine which color of apple is favored by your youngsters. Give each child three small pieces of apple: one from a red apple, one from a green apple, and one from a yellow apple. Ask her to taste each one and choose her favorite.

Construct a bulletin-board display to illustrate the results of the taste test. Cut three large, simple tree shapes from green and brown bulletin-board paper. Mount the trees on a bulletin board with a light blue paper background. Then duplicate the apple patterns on page 62 several times on red, green, and yellow construction paper. Cut out the apples and have each child choose an apple cutout in the color that corresponds to her favorite apple. Have her write her name on the cutout. After all the students have made their selections, place the yellow apple cutouts on one tree, the red apple cutouts on another tree, and the green apple cutouts on the third tree. Have students help you count the number of apples on each tree. Write the total for each tree on the trunk.

Then ask students to talk about the results. Mount a length of chart paper beside the apple trees. Write students' dictation as they discuss the results of the taste test. Encourage them to compare quantities of *more, less,* and *equal.*

There are more green apples than yellow apples.

There are less yellow apples than red apples.

The most favorite apple is the red apple.

Applesauce Stories

Incorporate cooking and language in this yummy activity. With one small group of students at a time, gather all the ingredients to create a simple blender applesauce recipe. For each group you will need a red apple, a green apple, a yellow apple, and small amounts of sugar, cinnamon, and water. Use a knife to peel and slice the three apples as students watch. Then let them assist you in placing the apple pieces in a blender and adding the sugar, cinnamon, and water. They'll be fascinated as they watch the blender turn the chunks of apple into creamy applesauce. Spoon the applesauce into individual cups for the students to eat.

Then have the group create a book illustrating the applesauce recipe. Assign each child one ingredient or tool that was used to prepare the recipe. Have him draw his item on a sheet of white drawing paper. Assist the children in placing the pictures in the correct order. Have them observe as you use a marker to write a label for the item on each page. Add a final page which reads "Applesauce!" Create a cover for the group's book with the title of their choice and all their names as authors. Repeat this process with the remaining groups of students.

Making Applesauce
by:
Philip, Joey, Allyssa, Erica, and Jeannine

a red apple

a little water

An "Apple-tizing" Tune

What's the next best thing to munching on apples? Singing about them!

Apples, Apples
(sung to the tune of "Twinkle, Twinkle, Little Star")

Apples juicy, apples round;
On the tree or on the ground.

Apples yellow, apples red,
Apple pie and juice and bread!

Apples crunchy, apples sweet;
Apples are so good to eat!

Apples Everywhere

After giving students a chance to taste apples and applesauce, direct their attention to the many other products made from apples. Ask students to brainstorm a list of apple products. Then duplicate and send home the checklist on page 62 with each child. This family project will have parents and children working together to determine the apple products kept at their houses. Discuss the results when the checklists are returned. Hey! We eat apple butter at my house, too!

reading the story, try the recipe at the back of the book for "Country Bear's Good Neighbor Cake." Encourage your little ones to be good neighbors by sharing the cake with a class next door. Add a few birthday candles to make this a grand finale to your Johnny Appleseed birthday fun.

An Imaginary Trip To The Orchard

Where *do* all those delicious apples come from? Read *Picking Apples And Pumpkins* by Amy and Richard Hutchings (Scholastic Inc.) to familiarize your little ones with how apples are picked at an orchard. Then take your students on an imaginary apple-picking adventure!

Counting On Apples

Sing this song to help your youngsters practice counting to ten. For added fun, give each child ten apple-shaped stickers. Have her place an apple sticker on each fingertip. Have her hold up the appropriate number of fingers as she sings.

Ten Little Apples
(sung to the tune of "Ten Little Indians")

One little, two little, three little apples,
Four little, five little, six little apples,
Seven little, eight little, nine little apples,
Ten little apples for you and me!

We
Have
Apples
Up
On
Top!

by
Ms. Hamrick's
Class

Kyle has 6
apples up on top.

More Apple Arithmetic

For more counting practice with an apple theme, share the story *Ten Apples Up On Top* by Theo. LeSieg (Random House, Inc.). This wild, rhyming story about critters who balance apples on their heads will have your students in stitches! After reading the story, create a class book your youngsters will want to read again and again.

For each page, you'll need a 7 1/4" x 28" piece of poster board (a standard sheet cut lengthwise into thirds). To prepare the book, program each page as shown and attach a head-and-shoulders photo of a child in your class. Then duplicate and cut out a large supply of construction-paper apples, using the patterns on page 62. Assign each child a number, beginning with one and going as high as the number of students in your class. (For a fun way to assign the numbers, write them on slips of paper; then have each student draw a slip from an apple-shaped basket.)

Each child then completes his page by counting out the assigned number of apple cutouts and gluing them to his page above the photo. (Children will need to stagger the apples for the higher numbers.) Assist each child in writing his name and the correct number in the blanks. If students are able, have them number the apples as well. Print the title "We Have Apples Up On Top" on a cover. Punch two holes in the top of each page, place them in numerical order, and bind the book with metal key rings.

A is for APPLE

ant

alligator

astronaut

acorn

acrobat

ape

©1996 The Education Center, Inc. • SEPTEMBER • TEC202

63

All About Apples

by *Stephanie*

Apples can be different colors.

1

...apart the booklet covers and pages, ...
booklets together. Have each child complete his booklet as follows.

Cover: Color the tree. Glue several red-hot cinnamon candies onto the tree to represent apples.
Page 1: Color the apples appropriately.
Page 2: Glue real apple seeds in the spaces provided.
Page 3: Draw a picture of your favorite apple product in the space provided.

Encourage little ones to take their booklets home to share with their families.

61

All About Apples

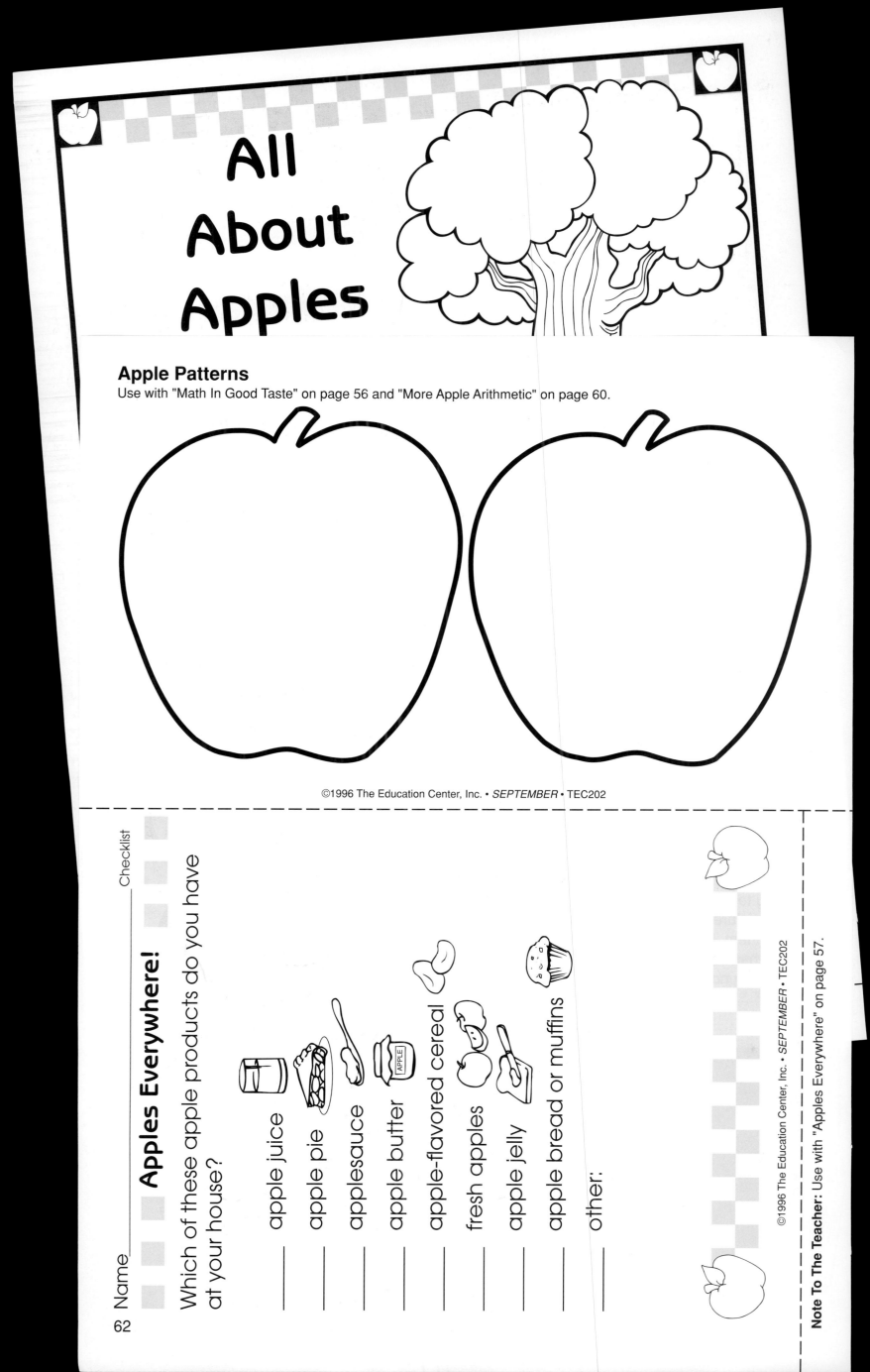

Apple Patterns
Use with "Math In Good Taste" on page 56 and "More Apple Arithmetic" on page 60.

©1996 The Education Center, Inc. • *SEPTEMBER* • TEC202

Name _____

Apples Everywhere!

Checklist

Which of these apple products do you have at your house?

_____ apple juice

_____ apple pie

_____ applesauce

_____ apple butter

_____ apple-flavored cereal

_____ fresh apples

_____ apple jelly

_____ apple bread or muffins

_____ other: _____

62

©1996 The Education Center, Inc. • *SEPTEMBER* • TEC202

Note To The Teacher: Use with "Apples Everywhere" on page 57.

There are seeds inside an apple.

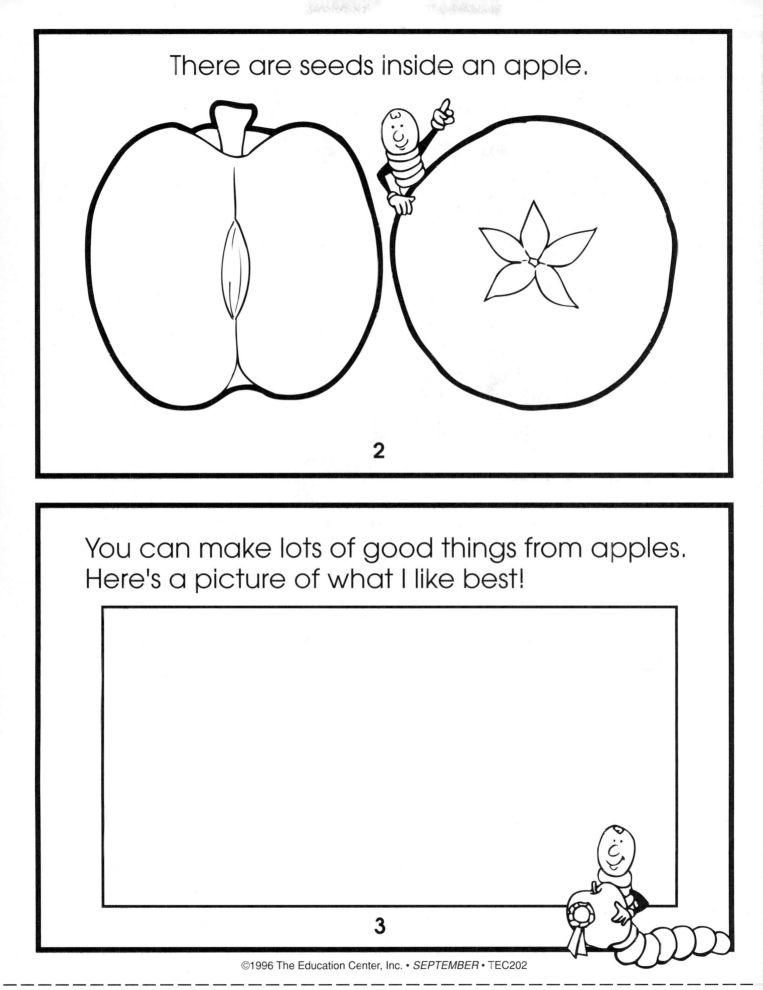

2

You can make lots of good things from apples.
Here's a picture of what I like best!

3

Note To The Teacher: Use these booklet pages with "All About Apples" on page 61.

Fun With Farm Animals

Amble down winding back roads to a rustic, hay-strewn, and animal-filled barnyard. Even if the journey is just an imaginary one, bushels of learning opportunities await your youngsters!

by Lucia Kemp Henry

Some Animals Live On A Farm

To get your youngsters to start thinking about the kinds of animals that are raised on farms, ask them to name animals. After each animal name is mentioned, ask the student whether that animal is likely to live on a typical farm. (Inevitably some really unusual animals—such as alligators, catfish, and ostriches—will be mentioned. Point out that these kinds of animals sometimes live on special and unusual kinds of farms!)

Make a list of the farm-animal names that your youngsters mention; then read and discuss a favorite farm-animal book. After your farmyard discussion, teach your youngsters a song that tells about some of the animals they have mentioned. After singing the verses given here, encourage youngsters to suggest other verses based on their farm-animal list.

On A Farm
(sung to the tune of "London Bridge Is Falling Down")

Animals live on a farm, on a farm, on a farm.
Animals live on a farm, with a farmer.

Cows and pigs live on a farm, on a farm, on a farm.
Cows and pigs live on a farm, with a farmer.

Goats and sheep live on a farm, on a farm, on a farm.
Goats and sheep live on a farm, with a farmer.

Hens and chicks live on a farm, on a farm, on a farm.
Hens and chicks live on a farm, with a farmer.

Animal Minipoems

Since young children love the rhythm and rhyme of poetry, these minipoems can be used for language play as well as to encourage an interest in reading. You can also use them as text for a big book, with student-created artwork illustrating each page.

A Horse
A horse can trot.
A horse can run.
A horseback ride
Is lots of fun!

Goats
Nanny goat, billy goat,
What do you say?
"Maa, maa." Silly goats,
Run away!

The Cow
The cow is big.
The cow says "moo."
The cow makes milk
For me and you.

Pigs
Pigs can oink.
Pigs can snort.
Pigs are fat
And kind of short.

Sheep
Sheep are quiet.
Sheep are cute.
Sheep give wool
To make a suit.

Geese
Geese can honk.
Geese can squawk.
Geese can fly
Or take a walk!

Old Rooster
Old Rooster woke up
Just so he could say,
"How do you cock-a-doodle
Do today?"

The Farm
The farm has a cow
And a horse and a pig.
And a sheep and a goat
And a barn **so** big!

Animal Art

Using an opaque projector and the animal patterns on page 73, you and your students can create some very large farm critters for a classroom mural. Enlarge each animal to the desired size on a different sheet of white bulletin-board paper. Divide your youngsters into small groups and have each group decorate its animal by sponge-painting it. Cut out each of the animals when the paint has dried; then attach each one to a bulletin board covered in green paper. Post a large word card on each animal.

If you're a bit more adventurous—especially if you have several helpful parent volunteers—use an opaque projector to enlarge each animal pattern onto cardboard. Have adult volunteers use X-acto® knives to cut out each design. Then have students sponge-paint the designs. If necessary, use markers to retrace paint-covered lines on each cutout. To make the cutouts self-standing, use packing tape to tape a sturdy weighted box to the back of each cutout. Place the cutouts in a corner with other farm-related props, and your little ones will flock to this barnyard to admire their work.

Get Real

During your farm-animal unit, provide opportunities for youngsters to get up close and personal with real farm animals. Perhaps a farm field trip is in order. Or perhaps a local farmer could bring a lamb, chicken, or other small farm animal to school for a visit. This time of year, many localities have fairs that feature petting zoos and livestock exhibits, so this may be a field-trip alternative worth pursuing.

When you have arranged to get the kids and the animals together, take lots of photographs. Allow plenty of time to discuss the sights, sounds, smells, and textures associated with each animal. You may even want to tape-record students' comments while they are experiencing the animals firsthand. Have enlargements made of the best of your photos, taking care to make your photo selection so that each child is included. Display each of the enlargements atop a bandanna attached to a bulletin board. Cut out a construction-paper speech balloon for each child, program it with something he said about a farm animal, and position it on the bulletin board so that onlookers can see who made the comment.

From The Farm To The Flannelboard

After your students have had some experiences with real, live farm animals, the animal patterns included in this unit can be used in a variety of ways. To create flannelboard cutouts, first photocopy pages 73 and 74 for later use. (If possible, make additional color photocopies of page 73 so that you can use them with other activities.) After removing page 73 from this book, glue it to a piece of tagboard. Laminate the designs before cutting out each one. Use craft glue to attach a square of felt to the back of each design. Place these flannelboard cutouts near your flannelboard where they can easily be used.

Additional uses for the patterns on page 73 are suggested in "Bodacious Booklet" on page 68, "A Grand Graph" and "Animal Sounds At Circle Time" on page 69, "Farm-Animal Friends" on page 70, and *Going To Sleep On The Farm* on page 71.

Bodacious Booklet

Help your youngsters assemble copies of this farm booklet that can be modified to match their ability levels. Reproduce the barn pattern on page 72 onto red construction paper for each child. Also, using white construction paper, reproduce the barn booklet cover and wheels on page 74 for each child. After you've used an X-acto® knife to cut along the dotted lines on each child's barn design, help him cut out his barn. Provide the child with a brad and a cut-out copy of one of the wheels on page 74. Help him attach the wheel to the back of the barn by punching the brad through the dot on the barn and then through the dot on the wheel. Spread the brad to hold the wheel in place.

Ask each child to cut out his copy of the booklet cover. For booklet pages, provide him with seven 5 1/2" x 4 3/4" pieces of white construction paper. Assist each child in stapling these pages and the booklet cover to the barn.

To have the children complete the art for each of the booklet pages, choose one of the following approaches:

- Using a photocopy of the farm-animal designs on page 73, have each child cut and paste an animal on each booklet page.
- Using shaped sponges that correspond with the animals on the wheel attached to the barn, have each child sponge-paint a different farm animal on each page.
- Help each youngster read the word showing through the opening in his barn. Have him draw a picture of the corresponding farm animal. To complete the subsequent pages, have him turn the wheel before drawing another animal.

Assist each youngster in completing his booklet by noting his comments about the animal illustrated on each page. Once the booklets are complete, encourage children to read their booklets to others. Mention that the booklet can be used as a matching game too. Whenever a student reads a booklet page, he can spin the wheel to display the matching animal word or picture.

What Farm Animals Need:

hay
grass
a barn
water

What Do Farm Animals Need?

During your farm-animal study, you may want to share books with your youngsters that show many barnyard scenes. Give students the opportunity to think about what they've seen that farm animals need to live and grow. List the needs mentioned on a barn-shaped cutout (see the pattern on page 75). As you discuss animal needs with students, be sure to mention that food, shelter, water, medical care, and even love or attention (from animal parents and humans) are necessary for healthy animals.

On another barn-shaped cutout, list related chores that must be done to meet the needs of farm animals as students brainstorm them. When this list is complete, ask each child which job he would most like to do and why.

Animals On The Farm by Joan

I like cows.

horse

This is a pig.

I want a horse.

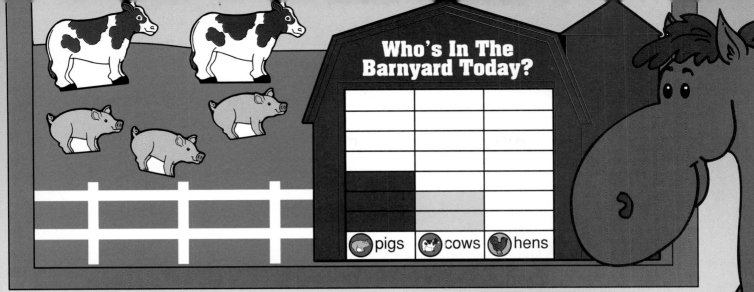

Who's In The Barnyard Today?

pigs cows hens

A Grand Graph

Use the large barn pattern on page 72 to construct a giant graph/poster that can be used in several different ways. Using an opaque projector, enlarge the barn design and trace it onto red bulletin-board paper. Cut out the design; then staple it to a bulletin board. Trim a sheet of white bulletin-board paper to fit the size of the barn-door opening. Draw a grid on this paper for the actual graph. Staple it to the barn. Program the graph with picture labels and titles in preparation for recording student responses to questions such as, "What's the cutest baby farm animal?" Use rectangles of different colors of construction paper (with students' names or photos) to complete the graph to correspond with students' responses.

To vary the use of this graph, replace the white paper if necessary. Visually fence off an area of the bulletin board. Each morning during your farm unit, post a different assortment of animals inside the fence. (Multiple copies of cutouts of the animal designs on page 73 may be useful for this purpose.) Have students count the animals and display the results on the graph.

Here Is The Barn

Have students rehearse this fingerplay first; then read aloud *Benjamin's Barn* by Reeve Lindbergh (Dial Books For Young Readers).

The Barn

Here is the barn	*Form a roof shape with your hands.*
Where I like to go.	*Walk in place.*
It's as tall as a tree	*Point up overhead.*
And cozy, you know.	*Hug body with arms.*
Here is the barn.	*Make a roof shape with your hands.*
I'll go there with you	*Walk in place.*
To pet a sweet lamb	*Pretend to pet a lamb.*
And cuddle it, too!	*Pretend to hug a lamb.*

Animal Sounds At Circle Time

Circle time is a fine time to play this lively animal-sound game. Make stick puppets from the farm-animal patterns on page 73, if desired, to accompany the activity. Teach your youngsters the following chant and have them recite it together.

> Down on the farm
> There is a cow.
> The cow says,
> "Moo, moo, moo!"

Repeat the chant several times, replacing the animal and the associated sound words to represent a different animal each time. If you made the stick puppets, have each youngster hold up the matching stick puppet as each animal is mentioned in the chant.

For a variation, chant the first two lines solo, omitting the animal name and holding up a stick puppet for a visual clue. Have youngsters finish out the chant with you and supply the sound of the animal you are holding.

Farm-Animal Friends

Plan a circle discussion as an introduction to this personalized painting project. Ask your youngsters to think about one farm animal that she especially likes and that she might want to raise as her own if she lived on a farm. Keep the discussion flowing by asking the following questions:

— Why do you like the animal that you have chosen?
— What would you do to take care of your animal?
— Where would you keep your animal?
— What would you name your animal?

On newsprint, have each child paint a large picture of the animal she has selected and cut it out when it has dried. (Younger children can finger-paint on paper using the color of their selected animals. Later, when the papers are dry, you can cut each one into the shape of the animal its painter selected. To make this step easier, use enlarged copies of the patterns on page 73 as tracers.) Ask each youngster to show her animal to the class and tell about it. If possible, take a photograph of each child with her animal.

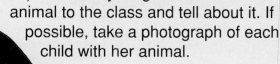

Farmers For A Day

Give your little ones the opportunity to be farmers for a day. Encourage students to come to school dressed for working on a farm. During your opening circle time, sing "The Farmer In The Dell." Change the verses to include your students' favorite farm animals. Later in the day, help students prepare farm-animal cookies using the preparation guidelines in "Critter Cookies."

The farmer in the dell, the farmer in the dell.
Hi-ho, the deery-oh, the farmer in the dell.
The farmer has a cow; the farmer has a cow.
Hi-ho, the deery-oh, the farmer has a cow.

Critter Cookies

Using some farm-animal cookie cutters, your students can create custom-designed cookies for snacktime. Prepare your favorite rolled cookie dough and add different ingredients for each kind of animal. For horses use a chocolate rolled cookie dough. To make pigs, tint cookie dough pink using a little red food coloring. To make sheep, use plain dough and sprinkle the baked cookies with coconut or sugar (or frost them). To make cows, use half plain dough and half chocolate dough. Mix the doughs together lightly for a marbled effect before rolling out the dough.

The Midnight Farm

Written by Reeve Lindbergh
Illustrated by Susan Jeffers
Published by Dial Books For Young Readers

As you read *The Midnight Farm* to your students, have them think about each kind of animal and discuss whether it is a pet, a farm animal, or a wild animal. Talk about the places where these three groups of animals pass the nighttime hours. Ask students to think about which group is found in the house, which group is found in the barn (stable or farmyard), and which group is found in the fields, near the pond and the trees. You might also discuss why all of the animals can't be in the house!

After you've completed a discussion of the story, read the following poem. Have your youngsters chant the last line of each verse in their most comforting good-night voices.

The Farm At Night

The farm at night is quiet and still.
The sun's put out its light.
And every creature on the farm
Has a place to spend the night.

Where is the cat, the cat, the cat?
Where is the cat at night?
The cat's in the warm and cozy house.
Oh, good night, cat, good night!
(Repeat verse for dog, boy, and girl.)

Where is the cow, the cow, the cow?
Where is the cow at night?
The cow's in the big and comfy barn.
Oh, good night, cow, good night!
(Repeat verse for horse, hen, and chick.)

Where is the deer, the deer, the deer?
Where is the deer at night?
The deer's in the green and quiet field.
Oh, good night, deer, good night!
(Repeat verse for mouse and fox.)

Going To Sleep On The Farm

Written by Wendy Cheyette Lewison
Illustrated by Juan Wijngaard
Published by Dial Books For Young Readers

This lovely book is just right for three- and four-year-old youngsters with its simple text and pretty, uncomplicated illustrations. As you read the book, have your little ones follow the example of the young boy in the story by putting small plastic farm animals to sleep in a toy barn or in a simple box covered with red paper. If you don't have plastic animals, use the flannelboard figures described in "From The Farm To The Flannelboard" on page 67. (The goose can be used as a duck and the rooster as a hen.) You can also make a flannelboard barn using the large barn pattern on page 72. Encourage youngsters to make quiet, sleepy animal sounds as you read the story.

'Til The Cows Come Home

Get your little ones moving—barnyard style—with this simply active game. First make cow-shaped tags using white, brown, and black construction paper and the cow pattern on page 73. Divide your youngsters into three groups. Select one set of colored cow tags for each group and tape a tag to each child's shirt. Specify a large, open area as an imitation barnyard. Mark a large, rectangular barn shape on the ground using jump ropes, colored tape, or yarn. Ask your youngsters to move around the barnyard just the way that cows might move. While the children are pretending to be cows, call one group to come into the barn by saying, "Brown cows, come home!" All of the brown cows must come into the marked-off barn shape before you release them to the pasture again. Call each color of cows to the barn several times before ending the game.

71

Pattern

Use with "Bodacious Booklet" on page 68, "A Grand Graph" on page 69, and *Going To Sleep On The Farm* on page 71.

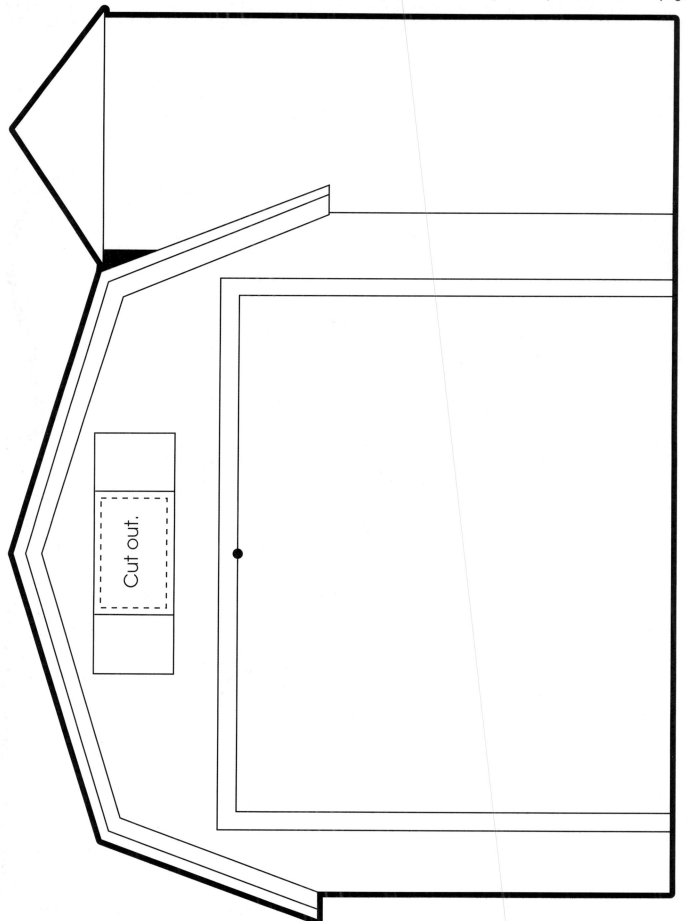

Cut out.

Farm-Animal Patterns

After photocopying page 74 for later use, use these designs with "Animal Art" and "From The Farm To The Flannel-board" on page 67, "Bodacious Booklet" on page 68, "Animal Sounds At Circle Time" on page 69, "Farm-Animal Friends" on page 70, and/or *Going To Sleep On The Farm* on page 71.

73

Patterns

Use wheels and booklet cover with "Bodacious Booklet" on page 68.

wheels

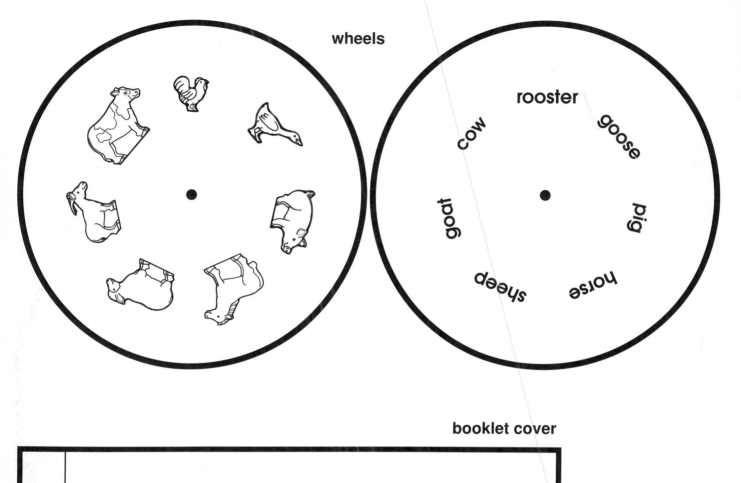

booklet cover

Animals On The Farm

by

VIVA MEXICO!

"Viva Mexico!" The jubilant cries of the crowd fill the *zócalos*—the public squares—of towns and cities across Mexico as the clock strikes 11 on the evening of September 15. So begin the national Independence Day festivities. Mexican Independence Day, September 16—*Diez y Seis de Septiembre*—commemorates the beginning of Mexico's fight for freedom against Spain. Celebrate the history and culture of Mexico with these activities that culminate in a traditional Mexican fiesta.

by Suzanne Moore

ANCIENT ARCHITECTURE

Mexico has many pyramids built by ancient Indian civilizations. Using a picture of a Mexican pyramid, engage students in a discussion about its shape and size. Point out that the pyramid tops in Mexico are flat. Entice your little ones to become pyramid architects using this sand play dough. To make enough dough for four to five students, put two cups of sand, one cup of cornstarch, and two teaspoons of alum in a large iron pot (or an old pot). Pour one cup of hot water into the pot; then stir the ingredients together over medium heat until the mixture reaches the consistency of dough. When it has cooled, divide the dough among the youngsters and invite them to form the dough into pyramids. After their pyramids dry—approximately three days—encourage youngsters to take them home to share with their families.

PATRIOTIC COLORS

The colors of the Mexican flag—green, red, and white—are abundant in the Independence Day decorations. In preparation for the celebration described in "Food, Fun, Fiesta!" on page 80, have youngsters make this windsock sporting Mexico's patriotic colors. Duplicate a class quantity of the patterns on pages 82 and 83. Around the rim of a white paper plate, have each child use red and green markers to create a decorative design. Have him color and cut out the two patterns; then glue them on opposite sides of his plate. Along the rim of the plate near the bottoms of the patterns, staple 36-inch lengths of green, red, and white crepe-paper streamers. To hang the windsock, punch two holes at the top of the plate. Thread one end of a length of yarn through both holes; then tie it securely. Hang the windsocks on a classroom window for display until the day of the fiesta.

ALL THAT GLITTERS...

Silver, gold, and copper are among the metals used by artists and jewelry makers in Mexico. Each youngster will enjoy the opportunity to role-play the part of a metalworker as he makes his own silver armband. For 24 hours, soak a classroom supply of tongue depressors in water; then carefully bend each one to fit into a coffee cup. When dry, remove each from its cup—the tongue depressor will retain its curved form. To make an armband, assist each child as necessary to cover his curved stick with a piece of aluminum foil. Using a pencil, have him etch designs on his armband. Invite each child to describe his designs to classmates. Afterwards store all of the armbands together for the activity "El Mercado" on page 80.

...IS SOMETIMES GOLD

In the streambeds of Mexico, gold nuggets were easily found by ancient Indians. Later, Mexicans taught gold-panning to the California prospectors of 1849. Make this streambed in your class sand table to give your little ones the chance to discover gold! To make gold nuggets, cover small pebbles or marbles with gold spray paint. Create a streambed by placing two inches of sand and the gold nuggets in the bottom of the sand table; then pour in water until the table is approximately half full. Provide each child with a deep-dish foil pie plate to use as a gold pan. Explain that he will fill his pan about three-fourths full with a scoop of the sand and water from the streambed. Then have him tilt the pan and swirl the water around so that the heavier materials—the gold—will sink to the bottom. Provide hand magnifiers and plastic tweezers for students to use in examining their precious nuggets. Before long, your delighted youngsters will be exclaiming, "I've discovered gold!"

GOBLETS AND CHOCOLATE

Ancient Aztecs made golden ornate goblets for serving a Mexican favorite—hot chocolate! Youngsters will enjoy the opportunity to make their own golden goblets for this tasty drink. For each child, provide a Styrofoam® cup and a gold or yellow crayon. Have him color the outside of the cup with the crayon. While coloring, encourage him to support the cup from the inside with his other hand. Set the completed goblets aside to use with "El Mercado" on page 80 and until the class has its "Food, Fun, Fiesta!" celebration (see page 80). At that time, serve a south-of-the-border version of hot chocolate to students in their goblets.

To make Mexican-style chocolate, have each student place the end of a *molinillo*—a special wooden beater—into his goblet of warm chocolate. Then, with his goblet held stable, have him spin the beater between his palms until his drink becomes foamy. If a molinillo is not available, assist each student in using a whisk or nonelectric beater to froth his chocolate. Supervise students closely during this activity to ensure correct use of the beater and to avoid spills and burns. For true Mexican flavor, invite students to sprinkle some cinnamon into their hot chocolate!

77

eyedropper per...
onto his coffee filter. Engage the students in a discussion about color combinations as the colors on their filters blend. After each filter dries, pinch and twist its center; then staple or wrap a short piece of pipe cleaner around it. Shape the filter to resemble a flower. If desired, staple a leaf cutout to the flower. On a large tagboard ring, mount the flowers close together to create a wreath. Display the wreath for the celebration described in "Food, Fun, Fiesta!" on page 80. ¡Qué bonito!

FABULOUS FIREWORKS

Fireworks are an important part of the Mexican Independence Day celebration. With this eye-popping activity, a brilliant fireworks display can be re-created right in your own classroom! Provide each student with a sheet of black construction paper and a straw. With an eyedropper put several drops of white tempera paint that has been thinned with water on each child's paper. Using his straw, have him blow the paint so that it spreads across the paper. Encourage the child to repeat the process, using thinned green and red paint. While the paint is wet, have him sprinkle glitter on it; then shake off the excess. When the paper has dried, cut the edges into random zigzags to resemble an exploding cascade of light. Display these sparkling explosives on your classroom walls to create a fireworks display.

79

INTERESTING IGUANA

The *iguana*, a native of Mexico, is a harmless vegetarian that lives in trees. An adult iguana can grow to be six feet long and weigh up to 18 pounds. As a pet, the iguana is quite interesting and enjoys doing unusual things such as perching on its owner's shoulder! For an enlightened tale about these lizards, read *The Iguana Brothers* by Tony Johnston (The Blue Sky Press). Afterwards encourage your little ones to make their own friendly iguanas with this activity. For each child, duplicate page 84. Cut a supply of toilet-tissue tubes in half lengthwise. Using green paint, have each child sponge-paint the iguana reproducible. After it dries, help him cut and then glue the iguana around a half-tube so that it appears to be standing. If desired, have the child embellish his iguana with green rickrack along its back.

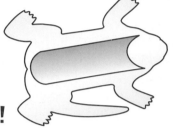

TACO TIME!

Mexican culture has made an impact in America in many different ways. American food has been influenced by the many traditional dishes introduced by Mexicans. One of the more popular ethnic foods adopted in this country is the taco. The familiar American version of a

EL MERCADO

In your housekeeping area, prepare a *mercado*, a Mexican market, so youngsters can shop for their celebration supplies for the "Food, Fun, Fiesta!" activities described on this page. From green, blue, and red construction paper, cut a large quantity of dollar-sized rectangles to be used as Mexican money. Decorate a sign labeled "El Mercado" with green, red, and white streamers. Hang the sign over the market area. If desired, suspend a sheet over the area to represent a tent. On tables and blankets spread over the floor, arrange precut felt tortillas, plastic fruits, and plastic vegetables. Also display the armbands and goblets made in "All That Glitters..." and "Goblets And Chocolate" (page 77) and the garments made in "What Shall I Wear?" (page 79). Have paper bags and baskets available for your little shoppers to place their purchases in. Encourage students to take turns as vendors and shoppers. Have each shopper find the merchandise he made in previous activities, then bargain with each vendor on the price of each item. Encourage him to count his Mexican money to pay for his purchases. After students complete their bargaining at the market, have them put on their Mexican garments and jewelry in preparation for the class fiesta.

FOOD, FUN, FIESTA!

The biggest gathering for Diez y Seis de Septiembre is in the square in Mexico City. Large crowds—as well as vendors selling toys, food, and hot chocolate—gather to celebrate Mexico's birthday. Traditionally dressed men and women are seen, as are strolling mariachi bands. Food, fun, and a fiesta are on the minds of all the participants. Invite both students and their parents (see note—page 82) to help create a class fiesta to celebrate Mexican culture with authentic-style tacos, hot chocolate, traditional dress, and music!

In Mexico, tacos are a favorite food, just as hamburgers and hot dogs are in the United States. The preparation of tacos in Mexico is different from that in the United States. There, a soft, hot tortilla is filled with meat or mashed beans. Then the tortilla is rolled up and eaten. Have students begin their class celebration by making a south-of-the-border taste sensation—Mexican-style tacos. For each student, provide a scoop of warm refried beans on a warm flour tortilla. Have him spread the beans on his tortilla, then roll the tortilla up and enjoy it! Afterwards ask students to sing the tune "Mucho Gusto Por Mí!" on page 78.

During the class fiesta, encourage your little ones to wear their Mexican clothing and jewelry. Prepare Mexican chocolate in the students' goblets as described in "Goblets And Chocolate" on page 77. Provide rhythm instruments as you play a version of the "Mexican Hat Dance" and other national tunes. Invite students to play and dance to the music. Suggest that they wave their windsocks made in "Patriotic Colors" (page 76) to show their national spirit. At the end of the celebration, have children view their fireworks display as you lead them in a jubilant cry of "Viva Mexico!"

TALES OF MEXICO

Use these literature selections to enhance your students' experiences with the culture of Mexico. For additional titles, reproduce a class quantity of the bookmark on page 83 for students to take home. Encourage your youngsters, during the next family trip to the library, to ask their parents to look for books listed on the bookmark.

by Mackie Rhodes

How Music Came To The World
retold by Hal Ober (Houghton Mifflin Company)

Find out if your youngsters know how music got its origins. After a brief discussion, read this myth aloud to share how Mexican legend explains the introduction of music to our world. Then, on the floor, tape a path to resemble a maze. At the end of the maze, place a box of rhythm instruments. In turn have one child follow the maze to the box. Have him select an instrument from the box, then return to his seat by retracing his steps along the maze. After all the instruments have been chosen, play some traditional Mexican recordings. Encourage the students to play their instruments to the rhythm of the music. Have those students without instruments keep the rhythm by clapping their hands, snapping their fingers, or stomping their feet. Repeat the activity to give every child an opportunity to follow the maze and play an instrument.

The Tale Of Rabbit And Coyote
by Tony Johnston (G. P. Putnam's Sons)

This Mexican folk story is a blend of several traditional stories. Throughout the story, the trickster Rabbit manages to escape even the most clever of traps by conning Coyote with his wily ways. But when Rabbit climbs a ladder to the moon, has he maneuvered himself into an inescapable trap? Will Coyote finally discover a way to avenge himself? After reading the story, have children recall some of Rabbit's tricks. Explain that in Mexican folklore, "the rabbit in the moon" is similar to the American version of "the man in the moon." For each child, duplicate page 85. Provide him with two shades of blue tissue paper. Encourage the child to tear his paper into small pieces. Have him roll the torn tissue paper into balls, then glue one shade of blue balls onto the rabbit and the other shade onto the moon. Have each child write or dictate an ending to the phrase, "If I were the rabbit in the moon, I would...."

If I were the rabbit in the moon, I would *jump up and touch all the stars*.

MORE MEXICAN TALES

Saturday Market
Written by Patricia Grossman
Published by Lothrop, Lee & Shepard Books

Count Your Way Through Mexico
Written by Jim Haskins
Published by Carolrhoda Books, Inc.

Abuela
Written by Arthur Dorros
Published by Dutton Children's Books

REFERENCES FOR TEACHERS

Fiesta! Mexico's Great Celebrations
Written by Elizabeth Silverthorne
Published by The Millbrook Press

Mexico: The Culture
Written by Bobbie Kalman
Published by Crabtree Publishing Company

Kids Explore America's Hispanic Heritage
Written by Westridge Young Writer's Workshop
Published by John Muir Publications

Windsock Pattern
Use with "Patriotic Colors" on page 76.

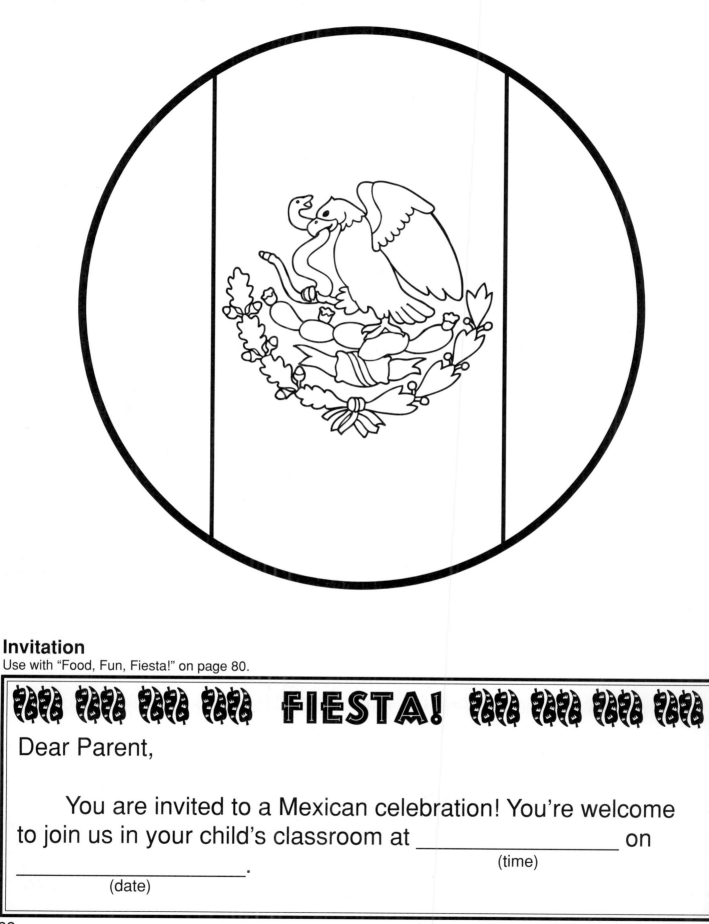

Invitation
Use with "Food, Fun, Fiesta!" on page 80.

🌶️🌶️🌶️🌶️ **FIESTA!** 🌶️🌶️🌶️🌶️

Dear Parent,

You are invited to a Mexican celebration! You're welcome to join us in your child's classroom at _____ on
(time)
_____.
(date)

©1996 The Education Center, Inc. • *SEPTEMBER* • TEC202

VIVA MEXICO!
DIEZ Y SEIS
DE SEPTIEMBRE

At Fiesta Time Or Siesta Time...
Share A Book With Your Child!

Lorenzo The Naughty Parrot
Written by Tony Johnston
Published by Harcourt Brace Jovanovich

Rain Player
Written by David Wisniewski
Illustrated by Elisa Kleven
Published by Clarion Books

A Birthday Basket For Tía
Written by Pat Mora
Published by Macmillan Publishing

Listen To The Desert: Oye Al Desierto
Written by Pat Mora
Published by Clarion Books

The Iguana Brothers
Written by Tony Johnston
Published by The Blue Sky Press

Iguana Pattern
Use with "Interesting Iguana" on page 78.

If I were the rabbit in the moon, I would _____

_____

_____.

Mother Goose's Nursery Rhymes

Children's love for nursery rhymes continues to flourish generation after generation. Use time-honored nursery rhymes and the ideas in this unit to bring new life to early-childhood activities.

by Deborah Burleson

There was a crooked man,
And he went a crooked mile.
He found a crooked sixpence
    beside a crooked stile.
He bought a crooked cat,
Which caught a crooked mouse,
And they all lived together
In a little crooked house.

Rhymes For Every Occasion

Ten nursery rhymes are featured in this theme unit. Each of these rhymes is printed on page 92, 94, or 96. Duplicate each rhyme on construction paper or tagboard for several different uses. Cut out the cards; then use them in any of the following ways:

— Read a card to the children to introduce a nursery rhyme and a related activity. If you have a goose puppet or care to make one from a white sock, use it to signal the introduction of a nursery rhyme.

— Give each student a copy of each newly introduced rhyme. Perhaps you'll want to punch a hole in each child's cards and fasten the set together with a binder ring or brad.

— Have one or more students illustrate each rhyme by painting a picture or by creating a collage of items that relates to the rhyme. When these masterpieces have dried, bind them into a booklet for your reading center.

— Paint a cube-shaped box a solid color or cover it with Con-Tact® paper. Attach a copy of each of six different nursery-rhyme cards to a different side of the box. When it's time to say nursery rhymes, have a child toss this giant die. The rhyme that lands faceup is the next one to be chanted!

The Crooked Mile

Start your nursery rhyme unit with some crooked antics based on the rhyme about the crooked man who went a crooked mile. Using colorful masking tape, make one or more zigzag paths on the floor of your classroom. Introduce the crooked man nursery rhyme using the reproducible on page 92. Show students the crooked path on your floor and have them demonstrate different ways to walk the path. During transition times, recite the rhyme as you lead students in walking along the crooked path. You might say, for example, "Let's all walk a crooked mile to get our coats!" Or for a large-motor activity, play some instrumental march music and encourage students to vary their arm and leg movements as they zig and zag down that crooked path.

Little Crooked Houses

Promote fine-motor control and mathematical concept development with a stack of 3" x 5" poster-board cards. Cut four one-inch slits in each card as shown. Place the cards at a table. Encourage students to use the cards to build crooked houses that would have brought a smile to the face of the crooked man.

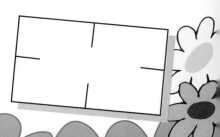

Mary, Mary, quite contrary,
How does your garden grow?
Silver bells and cockleshells,
And pretty maids all in a row.

Three little kittens
They lost their mittens,
And they began to cry,
Oh, Mother dear,
We sadly fear
Our mittens we have lost.
What! lost your mittens,
You naughty kittens!
Then you shall have no pie.
Mee-ow, mee-ow, mee-ow.
No, you shall have no pie.

Mistress Mary's Garden

If desired, use the Mary, Mary rhyme card on page 92 to lead each youngster in chanting the rhyme about Mary's garden. Then talk about what the rhyme means. Does Mary's garden have real bells, shells, and maidens in it? Probably not. If students don't arrive at this conclusion on their own, explain that Mary's garden probably had flowers that were shaped like bells, shells, and maidens. Show students pictures or photographs of flowers that have really interesting shapes. *Planting A Rainbow* by Lois Ehlert (Harcourt Brace Jovanovich) is a good resource for flower pictures.

To prepare for an art project inspired by Mary's garden, cut out copies of the bell- and shell-shaped patterns on page 96. Trace these patterns onto several compressed sponges and cut them out. Dampen the sponges; then have students take turns dipping them into shallow pans of tempera paint and pressing them onto a one- or two-foot-wide strip of white bulletin-board paper. When the paint has dried, use a wide house-painting brush to coat the area beneath and beside the sponge prints with thinned glue. Have students press randomly cut strips of varying shades of green construction paper or tissue paper onto the glue for stems and leaves. Your students' garden patch can be used as a bottom border on a bulletin board or to brighten up the hallway outside your classroom.

Kittens And Their Mittens

Everyone loves the three little kittens that lost their mittens! Ask some parent volunteers to help you collect fabrics and papers of different textures and cut them into mitten shapes of varying sizes. You will need lots of mitten cutouts for this activity. Introduce the rhyme to your students using the rhyme card on page 92. Then talk about mittens and their textures. Provide each youngster with glue and a piece of poster board. Have him select mitten cutouts of his choice and glue them to his poster board to create a collage. When his collage has dried, encourage him to talk about the textures of the mittens in his collage. This one is soft and silky, but this one is bumpy.

Designer Mittens

The kittens' mittens must have been very special to them. Encourage your children to design mittens that will be very special too. Give each child a large mitten shape cut from art paper. Provide glue and an assortment of sewing and craft notions. For example, you might supply pieces of yarn, scraps of wool, rickrack, small paper shapes or hole punches, gummed labels, stickers, and small magazine pictures. Ask each child to create an original mitten design. Interview volunteer mitten designers to find out what inspired their mitten creations.

This little piggy went to market;
This little piggy stayed home;
This little piggy had roast beef;
This little piggy had none;
And this little piggy cried,
"Wee, wee, wee, wee, wee!"
All the way home.

The Pig That Went To Market

With the nursery rhyme on page 92 and the full-color pig patterns on pages 93 and 95, your students will soon feel right at home. To prepare for this activity, first photocopy pages 94 and 96 for later use; then glue pages 93 and 95 to tagboard and laminate them. Cut out each pig before attaching a square of felt to its back. Introduce "This Little Pig Went To Market" to your students; then have students take turns using the flannelboard cutouts to illustrate the action. Have each child take a turn selecting three of the pigs. Of the three, have him indicate which is largest, which is smallest, and which is medium- or middle-sized in comparison. Encourage students to use the pig flannelboard figures during their free-play time.

Little Miss Muffet sat on a tuffet,
Eating her curds and whey.
Along came a spider,
Who sat down beside her,
And frightened Miss Muffet away.

Miss Muffet Pigs Out

Miss Muffet isn't into roast beef. It's curds and whey—cottage cheese—that strikes her fancy. Introduce your youngsters to Miss Muffet, using the reproducible on page 94 if desired. Talk about what Miss Muffet was eating. Find out if any of your youngsters have ever eaten curds and whey. Then explain that this yummy recipe is one great way to prepare curds (cottage cheese) for snacktime. Let the cooking begin!

Miss Muffet's Delight

1 small package orange or lime Jell-O® (dry)
1 12 oz. container frozen nondairy whipped topping (thawed)
1 pint of small-curd cottage cheese
1 6 oz. can crushed pineapple (drained)
1 cup miniature marshmallows

Spoon cottage cheese and whipped topping into a large bowl. Sprinkle on dry Jell-O®. Stir until well blended. Fold in pineapple and marshmallows. Chill 20 minutes before serving.

Little Boy Blue, come blow
    your horn!
The sheep's in the meadow,
The cow's in the corn.
Where is the boy who looks
    after the sheep?
He's under the haystack,
Fast asleep.

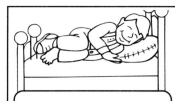

Diddle, diddle, dumpling,
    my son John,
Went to bed with his trousers on;
One shoe off, and one shoe on,
Diddle, diddle, dumpling,
    my son John.

Diddle, Diddle, Dumpling

My son John went to bed with his trousers on. One shoe off and one shoe on. Diddle, diddle, dumpling, my son John. (See the reproducible on page 94.) Have students speculate about why John went to bed with one shoe on. Then explain that for a few minutes, each of them is to pretend to be John. Ask each student to remove one shoe. Place all the shoes in a pile and have students sit in a circle around the pile, pretending to sleep. On your signal, have each student wake up, rush to the pile to find her shoe, slip the shoe on (no need to buckle or tie), and return to her place in the circle. As you are assisting students in refastening their shoes, find out which shoes they think are the easiest to fasten and which are the hardest to fasten. Also discuss the colors, shapes, and various sizes of the shoes that students are wearing.

The Search For Little Boy Blue

Where is that Little Boy Blue? Well, as the rhyme on page 94 has it, he's under a haystack fast asleep! After reciting Little Boy Blue's nursery rhyme several times, ask students to think of other things Little Boy Blue could have been doing when he was discovered. Could he have been petting a dog or singing a song? Ask each child to draw a picture of something Little Boy Blue could have been doing under the haystack. Then provide each child with a tabbed haystack cutout like the one shown. While a child is gluing straw or yellow paper strips to cover all of his haystack cutout—except the tab—use an X-acto® knife to cut a slit above the drawing. (Position the slit so that the haystack will cover the drawing when the tab is inserted in it.) When the haystack is complete, have the child insert the tab in the slit and bend the haystack to cover the drawing. Tape the tab to the back of the paper to hold it in place. To give each student an opportunity to introduce his new version of the rhyme, repeatedly say the verse. Each time, have a different child supply the last line and lift the flap to show what's going on under his haystack.

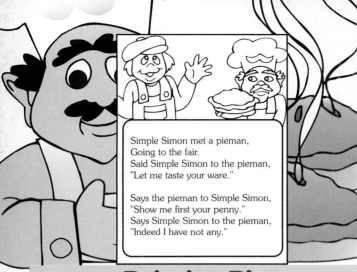

Simple Simon met a pieman,
Going to the fair.
Said Simple Simon to the pieman,
"Let me taste your ware."

Says the pieman to Simple Simon,
"Show me first your penny."
Says Simple Simon to the pieman,
"Indeed I have not any."

Painting Pies

Read aloud "Simple Simon" on page 96. Then invite your students to make some pretend pies. First invert two stacked paper plates over two others so that all four plates are rim-to-rim. Staple the plates together all the way around. You will need one of these pie forms for each student.

Pie-Paint Recipe

1 cup white flour
1 cup wheat flour
1/4 tsp. ground cloves
1/4 tsp. nutmeg or ginger
2 teaspoons cinnamon
2 cups water

Combine the ingredients in a bowl, mixing well. This makes enough sweet-smelling pie paint for 10 to 12 pies, so you may want to make two batches of the recipe, depending on your class size. Have each child paint a crust on the top half of his pie form, using a paintbrush. Allow the paint to dry for at least 24 hours. When the paint is dry, place each pie form in a different aluminum pie pan. With all these pies around, students will slip naturally into the roles of piemen, like the one that Simple Simon met. Just in case this pielike fragrance is too much for your children, it's a good idea to bake or serve a pie they can *really* sink their teeth into.

90

Pie Factory

While Simple Simon and the pieman are still fresh on your students' minds, put a few of the pies described in "Painting Pies" in your housekeeping or dramatic play area. Also include extra pie tins of various sizes, rolling pins, plastic utensils, aprons, chef hats (made from cuffed paper sacks), and play dough. Add to the fun by adding some peppermint oil to your play dough. Oh, my! Everyone will want to make pie. Where is that Simple Simon, anyway? We need to sell some pies!

Baa, baa, black sheep,
 have you any wool?
Yes, sir, yes, sir, three bags full:
One for my master, and one
 for my dame,
One for the little boy who
Lives down the lane.

Three Bags Full

As your students can tell when you share "Baa, Baa, Black Sheep" on page 94, that sheep is awfully proud of his wool. If you know of someone who lives nearby who could tell students about sheep shearing or how the wool is transformed into clothing, invite him or her to talk to your students and show them what wool looks like at different stages of the process. Later produce three drawstring or paper bags filled with woolen articles of clothing and pairs of wool fabric swatches. Have the students touch and discuss each object as it is brought out of a bag. Encourage children to find the swatches that match.

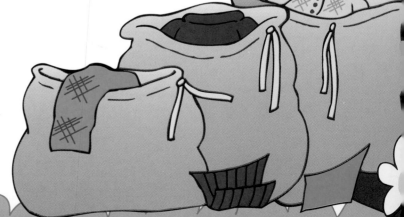

What Wee Willie Sees

Use the reproducible on page 96 to share with your youngsters the rhyme about Wee Willie Winkie. Solicit your students' assistance in making a nighttime bulletin board that features each of their families. To begin cut several house-shaped outlines from black construction paper. Use the house pattern on page 43 or cut several different shapes of houses for variety. You will need one house per child. Cover a bulletin board with dark blue paper and attach the houses along the bottom border. Ask each student to draw or attach pictures of his family on yellow paper squares sized to be windows for his house. Attach each child's family pictures to his house. To complete the board, have students attach self-adhesive foil stars and a moon to the blue background paper.

Wee Willie Winkie runs through the town,
Upstairs, downstairs in his nightgown;
Rapping at the window, crying through the lock,
"Are the children all in bed? Now, it's eight o'clock."

Wee Willie Has Rhythm

Wee Willie is just the person to inspire a little counting practice. Supply each child with rhythm sticks. Have children tap out the rhythm of the nursery rhyme as you repeatedly chant it together. Each time, end the nursery rhyme by mentioning a different hour. When the hour is called, have each child tap and count out that number. (If desired, you may want to display a clock set to the matching time.) Are the children all in bed? It's now six o'clock! One! Two! Three! Four! Five! Six!

Rhymes To Go

Parents who may not be in the habit of reciting nursery rhymes will be pleased when you send home a recording of your students chanting the rhymes they have learned. Tape-record your students saying some rhymes. Make a few copies of this recording. Let the children take turns checking out a tape (and if necessary, a tape player). Every now and then, play a copy of the tape during naptime, snacktime, or circle time.

There was a crooked man,
And he went a crooked mile.
He found a crooked sixpence
    beside a crooked stile.
He bought a crooked cat,
Which caught a crooked mouse,
And they all lived together
In a little crooked house.

Three little kittens
They lost their mittens,
    And they began to cry,
Oh, Mother dear,
We sadly fear
    Our mittens we have lost.
What! lost your mittens,
You naughty kittens!
    Then you shall have no pie.
    Mee-ow, mee-ow, mee-ow.
    No, you shall have no pie.

Mary, Mary, quite contrary,
    How does your garden grow?
Silver bells and cockleshells,
    And pretty maids all in a row.

This little piggy went to market;
This little piggy stayed home;
This little piggy had roast beef;
This little piggy had none;
And this little piggy cried,
"Wee, wee, wee, wee, wee!"
All the way home.

This little piggy stayed home.

HOME SWEET HOME

This little piggy went to market.

Little Miss Muffet sat on a tuffet,
Eating her curds and whey.
Along came a spider,
Who sat down beside her,
And frightened Miss Muffet away.

Little Boy Blue, come blow
your horn!
The sheep's in the meadow,
The cow's in the corn.
Where is the boy who looks
after the sheep?
He's under the haystack,
Fast asleep.

Diddle, diddle, dumpling,
my son John,
Went to bed with his trousers on;
One shoe off, and one shoe on,
Diddle, diddle, dumpling,
my son John.

Baa, baa, black sheep,
have you any wool?
Yes, sir, yes, sir, three bags full:
One for my master, and one
for my dame,
One for the little boy who
Lives down the lane.

This little piggy had roast beef.

This little piggy had none.

And this little piggy cried,
"Wee-wee-wee-wee!"
All the way home.

Nursery-Rhyme Reproducibles

Use with the nursery-rhyme activities on page 86 and pages 90–91.

Simple Simon met a pieman,
Going to the fair
Said Simple Simon to the pieman,
"Let me taste your ware."

Says the pieman to Simple Simon,
"Show me first your penny."
Says Simple Simon to the pieman,
"Indeed I have not any."

Wee Willie Winkie runs through
the town,
Upstairs, downstairs in his
nightgown;
Rapping at the window,
crying through the lock,
"Are the children all in bed?
Now, it's eight o'clock."

Bell And Shell Patterns

Use with "Mistress Mary's Garden" on page 87.